p. 95

Passages to America

Passages to America

Oral Histories of Child Immigrants from
Ellis Island and Angel Island

Emmy E. Werner

Potomac Books, Inc.
Washington, D.C.

Library of Congress Cataloging-in-Publication Data
Werner, Emmy E.
  Passages to America : oral histories of child immigrants from Ellis Island and Angel Island / Emmy E. Werner. — 1st ed.
      p. cm.
  Includes bibliographical references.
  ISBN 978-1-59797-296-3 (hardcover : alk. paper)
  1. Immigrant children—United States—History—20th century. 2. United States—Emigration and immigration—History—20th century. 3. Ellis Island Immigration Station (N.Y. and N.J.) 4. Angel Island Immigration Station (Calif.) I. Title.
  JV6600.W47 2009
  305.23092′273—dc22

                                                          2009012772

Printed in the United States of America on acid-free paper that meets the American National Standards Institute Z39-48 Standard.

Potomac Books, Inc.
22841 Quicksilver Drive
Dulles, Virginia 20166

First Edition

10 9 8 7 6 5 4 3 2 1

For Margaret Robinett and Stanley Jacobsen—with love—
and in memory of Robert William Robinett

Contents

Acknowledgments

My thanks go to Dr. Janet Levine, oral historian, who kindly provided me with interview transcripts from the Ellis Island Oral History Project, and to Barry Moreno and Jeff Dosik from the Ellis Island Research Library who graciously shared a selection of photos from the National Park Service with me.

I thank Marilyn Ibach from the Prints and Photograph Division of the Library of Congress, Washington, D.C., and the staff of the Still Pictures Department of the National Archives in College Park, Maryland, for photos of child immigrants. The financial support from the University of California's Washington Center for my travel and research in the nation's capital is gratefully acknowledged.

Daniel Necas from the Immigration History Research Center at the University of Minnesota provided copies of interviews with displaced persons who settled in the Midwest. The Pacific Regional Humanities Center at the University of California at Davis gave me access to selected cases from the Angel Island Oral History Project as did Erika Gee of the Angel Island Immigration Station Foundation. I thank them all.

My husband, Stanley Jacobsen, descendant of immigrants from Denmark, Alsace, and Armenia, used his superb research and computer skills to locate information about child immigrants from all over the world and patiently typed my manuscript. I thank him and my editor, Elizabeth Demers, for their steadfast emotional support and wise counsel.

Introduction

In the East Wing of the Ellis Island Immigration Museum stands the statue of a young Irish girl, holding onto her hat and carrying a bag with all her earthly possessions. Her name is Annie Moore, and she was the first immigrant to enter Ellis Island on January 1, 1892. She arrived on her fifteenth birthday, which was also the opening day of the new Immigration Station in New York. More than twelve million "aliens" passed through its Registry Room until the station closed in November 1954.[1]

The Irish lass came with two younger brothers—Anthony, age eleven, and Philip, age seven. The three children had sailed from Queenstown, County Cork, to America in steerage aboard the steamship *Nevada*. Their parents and an older brother had left Ireland three years earlier to find work in New York.

Annie, Anthony, and Philip were the first of more than two million child immigrants who went through Ellis Island during the next six decades. Accompanied by parents, siblings, cousins, or older relatives, the immigrant children came with bundles, boxes, and battered suitcases. Some orphans and stowaways traveled alone. Three hundred and fifty-five babies were born on Ellis Island; some fourteen hundred children died there in detention. For many, the station was the Island of Hope; for some, it became the Island of Tears.

This book tells the story of their American odyssey. The child immigrants' personal narratives offer a unique perspective on the lifelong process of gaining an "American" identity—its joys and sorrows, its promises and achievements—and the challenges and obstacles they encountered along the way.

Most of the stories in this book come from the archives of the Ellis Island Oral History Project, which is dedicated to preserving the immigrants' firsthand recollections of coming to America during the years Ellis Island was in operation. The archives contain information concerning everyday life in the immigrants' country of origin, their family history, their reasons for immigrating, their experiences on the journey to America, their processing in the immigration facilities, and an in-depth look at their adjustment to living in the United States. This information is accessible to the public for research.[2]

The personal narratives in this book include interviews with individuals who came to America during their formative years from countries that provided the greatest influx of immigrants to Ellis Island. Among them were youngsters from the British Isles (England, Wales, Ireland, and Scotland), Jewish refugees from Poland and Russia, immigrants from Italy and the Scandinavian countries, survivors of the Armenian genocide, German children who emigrated during the Great Depression, Jewish children who fled Hitler's regime, and displaced persons from Europe who were admitted to the United States after World War II.

The child immigrants ranged from four to sixteen years of age when they arrived on Ellis Island, but most were in their early teens. They were in their sixties, seventies, and eighties—their median age was seventy-seven—when they told their stories to the interviewers from the National Park Service.

A complementary perspective comes from the child immigrants who passed through the Angel Island Immigration Station located in San Francisco Bay. From 1910 to 1940, that station processed more than one million people coming to the United States from the Pacific Rim, that is, from China, Japan, India, and the Philippines. Since many of the immigrant inspectors there had transferred from New York, Angel Island became known as the "Ellis Island of the West."

With the passage of the Chinese Exclusion Act in 1882, the only federal legislation to ban a specific ethnic group's entry to the country, Angel Island became a detention and interrogation center for an estimated 175,000 would-be immigrants from China. The majority were "paper sons" or "paper daughters" who had purchased false identities in order to find new opportunities in America. Angel Island's board of special inquiry instituted long and arduous interrogations to check the veracity of the young immigrants' and their sponsors' testimonies.

Some youngsters on Angel Island faced long periods of detention. Immigrants carved beautiful Chinese calligraphy on the walls of their segregated barracks to express their hopes, fears, and feelings of sadness. Included in this book are the stories of boys who were ten to thirteen years old when they arrived and finally succeeded in their journey to *Gum Saan* (the Gold Mountain, or America). Students from the University of California collected their tales, as part of the Angel Island Oral History Project, giving us a firsthand account of their trials and triumphs in America.[3]

A new wave of child immigrants reached America's shores in the last three decades of the twentieth century. Most came from Latin America and Asia and some from Africa. Many were refugees from revolutions and civil wars; some were survivors of ruthless "ethnic cleansing." Among a growing number of unaccompanied minors were child refugees from Cuba, Haiti, and Central America. Among recent arrivals from Asia were the Vietnamese "boat people," the children from the Killing Fields of Cambodia, and the Hmong from the highlands of Laos. They were followed by the Lost Boys of Sudan, and Ethiopia, orphans of decades of civil war in Africa.[4]

Like the immigrants who came before them—and despite their diversity in cultural backgrounds—these newcomers are highly concentrated within America's major metropolitan areas. The final chapters in this book will assess the similarities and differences between the challenges these young immigrants face today and the resources child immigrants of previous generations used to successfully overcome adversities along their way. Despite encountering periodic anti-immigrant sentiments in the United States, their collective stories should make us proud of the young sojourners in our midst who came from all corners of the earth to make America their home.

1

Passing Through Ellis Island

Prior to 1855, there were no immigration stations in America. Newcomers to the "Promised Land" got off a boat and took their chances, as did thirteen-year-old Mary Chilton, the first passenger on the *Mayflower* who stepped ashore at Plymouth Rock on December 26, 1620. Fewer than half of the English colonists who arrived on that ship survived the first brutal winter in America. Mary buried her parents soon after they reached the new land.[1]

In the years to come, a steady stream of children followed the Pilgrims and crossed the Atlantic. Some came involuntarily: in the seventeenth century, vagrant children from the streets of London and Amsterdam were shipped to Virginia and New York and became indentured servants, and in the eighteenth century, children from the West Coast of Africa were brought to the American colonies and sold as slaves.

Among the first great waves of immigrants from Northern Europe who arrived after the American colonies gained their independence and before the Civil War were young people from England, Ireland, Scotland, Germany, and France. During the potato famine of 1845–49, many Irish children fled with their families on "coffin ships." Other children, recruited by the Latter-day Saints in

1

England, Scotland, and Scandinavia, crossed the Atlantic to find their earthly Zion in the wilderness of Utah.[2]

* * *

In the mid-nineteenth century, the U.S. government saw the need to exert some control over the influx of millions of newcomers and to deny entrance to "aliens" it deemed undesirable. In August 1855, Castle Garden in New York was designated the first immigration center. Eight million immigrants were processed there during the next four decades. Then, on January 1, 1892, the newly established U.S. Bureau of Immigration opened Ellis Island as the country's main immigration facility.

By the time Annie Moore, her brothers, and more than a hundred other passengers from the steamship *Nevada* arrived at Ellis Island at 11:00 a.m. on New Year's Day 1892, the Immigration Act of 1891 had become the law of the land. All mentally disabled persons, convicts, those who might become public charges, and those who suffered from a "loathsome or contagious disease" were refused admission to the United States of America. The Moore children were lucky. They could read and write English, were hale and hearty, and had their parents in the waiting area, below the Registry, to vouch for them.

To commemorate her arrival on the day of Ellis Island's official opening, Superintendent of Immigration Col. John B. Weber presented Annie with a ten-dollar gold coin. He also wished her good luck and a happy New Year. The next day the New York newspapers duly noted the event. Wrote a reporter in the *New York Herald* on January 2, 1892: "In less than half an hour from the time she landed [Annie Moore] was on the way to the City to spend the rest of New Year's Day."

Not all immigrant children were processed as quickly as Annie Moore and her brothers. Most of the young people who came during the next six decades traveled in steerage, or third class. They were all required to go to Ellis Island for more extensive processing after their steamships had docked at a Manhattan pier. All steerage passengers were put on a ferry and taken directly to the immigration station, where they underwent medical and legal examinations. For the vast majority the processing took between three and five hours.

Upon arrival, men were segregated from the women and children and lined up separately for inspection, by physicians of the U.S. Public Health Service. Children were detained at Ellis Island when they were sick and had to be hospitalized. Illnesses for which they were confined included chicken pox, diphtheria, measles, mumps, scarlet fever, tuberculosis, and trachoma. But it was also possible that another family member, either a parent or another relative in the party, might be the cause of delay at the station. In this case, the whole family was temporarily detained. Women and children traveling alone were always held until a male relative came for them.

Detention was a scary time for immigrants. Detainees would wait days, weeks, and even months before they found out whether they could stay in America. To make the detainees' lives more bearable the Bureau of Immigration relied on missionaries, social workers, and volunteers from the Hebrew Aid Society, Catholic and Protestant churches, the Salvation Army, and the Young Men's Christian Association (YMCA). Help came in many forms, but what mattered most was the ability to communicate with the immigrants in their languages and to allay their fears as best as possible.[3]

The Bureau of Immigration set up a rooftop garden on the main building of Ellis Island. Another was eventually set up in the baggage and dormitory building. An outdoor playground had a sandbox, two slides, and swings. Language, nationality, or race did not pose a barrier for the immigrant children who played together, even if they couldn't understand each other.

Schoolrooms and kindergartens for the youngest immigrants operated through the years on a voluntary basis. The "head" of the school or her assistant went through the detention rooms each weekday morning and afternoon, and the children who wished to attend school formed a line when she appeared. From the unlocked gate leading out of the detention rooms, the children were taken up a flight of stairs to the school and its rooftop playground. Many learned their first words of English there. Children aged ten to fourteen predominated in the classrooms.

The school at Ellis Island was used as a testing ground in a psychological study of immigrant children during the summers of 1922 and 1923. Bertha M. Boody, a psychologist, administered a range of nonlanguage tests (mostly items drawn from the Stanford-Binet Intelligence Test) to some three hundred youngsters, including children from Italy, Germany, and Poland as well as Jewish and

Armenian children. She noted in her monograph that "individual differences there are . . . but the curves of the scores in the different 'races' seem not to differ in any marked degree . . . from the curves shown in studies of unselected groups of American children. . . . The Ellis Island children show by no means an unfavorable comparison."[4]

The happiest time for most immigrant children held in detention was Christmas. The Great Hall that served as the Registry Room was decked out with an enormous Christmas tree, decorated with angel ornaments and a glittering star on the topmost branch. Missionary societies sent toys and fruit for the children. Girls received gaily printed cotton bags containing a doll, a towel, a washcloth, soap, a game, a set of toy dishes, three handkerchiefs, a writing tablet, a pencil box, and a pair of stockings. Boys received similar bags, with a game or small toys substituted for the doll. A musical program on Christmas Day featured social service workers dressed in native costumes singing English, German, Polish, Spanish, and Czech carols. Jewish children also celebrated their holidays: Passover, Yom Kippur, Sukkoth, and Hannukah. Their meals came from a kosher kitchen that was supervised by a rabbi.

In the end, most children in detention were approved to enter the country. With their mothers they would crowd in the Temporary Detention Room of the Discharging Division. Some waited for a relative to fetch them, others for money, and still others for the confirmation of an address. Some would meet their fathers for the first time in the Statue of Liberty's shadow.

Between 1892 and 1923, the immigration laws of the United States were relatively liberal. The "golden door" of Ellis Island was open with few restrictive laws. But the National Origins Act of 1924 limited admission to 2 percent of each immigrant nationality living in the United States in 1890. This quota system tended to favor old immigrant nationalities, such as the British, German, Irish, and Swedes, over the new immigration waves of Italians, Jews, and eastern Europeans.

The hardest quota cases were those that separated families. When a member of the family had been born in a country with a quota still open while another had been born in a country whose quota was exhausted, the law let in the first and deported the latter.

HENRY CURRAN, an Ellis Island commissioner from 1922 to 1926, relates his experience in dealing with the admission of a two-day-old infant, born at sea:

The Polish wife of a Pennsylvania coal miner, admitted a year before, had gone back to Poland to visit her old father and mother who had taken sick. The visit over, she returned quickly to America. She would be admitted at once, for short visits do not count against quotas. The coal miner was at the island, waiting for her. . . . Then the ship came in, the *Lapland* of the Red Star Line, from Antwerp. . . . On the day before the ship made port, out on the high seas, a baby had been born to the returning mother. . . . "Mother and child both doing well" in the Ellis Island hospital, everybody delighted— until the inspector admitted the mother but excluded the baby.

"Why?" asked the father, trembling.

"Polish quota exhausted," pronounced the helpless inspector. They brought the case to me. Deport the baby? I couldn't. . . . "The baby was not born in Poland," I ruled, "but on a British ship. She is chargeable to the British quota. The deck of a British ship is British soil, anywhere in the world."

"British quota exhausted yesterday," replied the inspector. . . .

"Come to think of it, the *Lapland* hails from Antwerp," I remarked. "That's in Belgium. Any ship out of Belgium is merely a peripatetic extension of Belgian soil. . . . Use the Belgian quota." So I directed.

"Belgian quota ran out a week ago." Thus, the inspector and I were stumped.

"Oh, look here," I began again. . . . "I've got it! How could I have forgotten my law so soon? You see, with children, it's the way it is with wills. We follow the intention. Now it is clear enough that the mother was hurrying back so the baby would be born here and be a native-born American citizen, no immigrant business at all. And the baby had the same intention, only the ship was a day late and that upset everything. But—under the law, mind you, under the law—the baby, by intention, was born in America. It is an American baby—no baby Pole at all— no British, no Belgian—just good American.

"That's the way I rule—run up the flag!"

The work of the Immigration and Naturalization Service (INS) on Ellis Island began to change when the government assigned the processing of aliens to U.S. consulates. By 1931, all questioning and medical examinations had to be completed at American consulates abroad before immigrants could be granted a visa allowing them to enter the United States. The number of child immigrants to the United States dropped dramatically from a high of 158,621 in 1914 to approximately 4,131 in 1933, and sank to even lower levels after America entered World War II.[5]

During World War II until Ellis Island's closure in 1954, the station was used chiefly as a place to detain enemy aliens and admit stateless refugees. In June 1948 Congress passed the Displaced Persons Act, which permitted the admission of up to 400,000 displaced persons during a two-year period, beginning July 1, 1948, with the numbers chargeable against future years' quotas. It was aimed at reducing the problems created by the presence in Germany, Austria, and Italy of more than one million displaced persons.

The Immigration Act of 1965 finally abolished the preferential quota system based on the immigrants' national origins. It introduced a new kind of preference quota that favored relatives of U.S. citizens, permanent alien residents, and refugees and set the stage for the next great wave of immigration from Latin America and Asia.

That same year, on May 11, President Lyndon B. Johnson proclaimed Ellis Island a part of the Statue of Liberty National Monument. Twenty-five years later, in 1990, a restored main building reopened to the general public as a museum. Millions of visitors now pass through the Great Hall each year and glance at the statue of the young Irish girl who was "first in line" for America. It is a gift of the Republic of Ireland to the people of the United States.

2

First in Line: Child Immigrants from the British Isles

After being united with her parents on New Year's Day 1892, Annie Moore and her brothers went off to their new home on Manhattan's Lower East Side. She married the son of a German-born baker at St. James Church in 1895. They had eleven children, five of whom survived to adulthood. She died of heart failure in 1924 at age forty-seven and is buried with six of her children at Calvary Cemetery in Queens. Among her living descendants are great-great grandchildren with Irish, German, Italian, and Scandinavian surnames, among them an investment counselor and a great-granddaughter with a Ph.D.[1]

After Annie Moore and her two younger brothers arrived, more than 3 million immigrants from the British Isles entered the United States between 1892 and 1954, representing one of the largest immigrant groups of the twentieth century. Approximately 1.3 million came from England, 1.1 million came from Ireland, some 600,000 from Scotland, and about 53,000 came from Wales.[2]

In the decade after World War I ended, as the Great Depression swept across Europe, many British war veterans left with their families and young children in search of better economic opportunities. Usually, they found a sponsor among relatives who had immigrated

earlier—an uncle or aunt who had already settled in the States or
an older brother who had found a job and established a family in
the new country. Most child immigrants from the British Isles who
passed through Ellis Island would see familiar faces upon their arrival: uncles, aunts, and cousins who spoke their language and who
would introduce them to the customs of their adopted land.

* * *

KATHLEEN EASON HARLOW was only four years old when she accompanied her parents from Great Britain to the United States in 1920.[3]
She treasured a book of children's stories that her aunt gave her as
a parting gift and a five-pound tin of Huntley & Palmers' biscuits
that her mother took along because Kathleen was a fussy eater. Their
ship, the *Carmania*, dodged icebergs all the way across the Atlantic.

> I was so short and little that I was usually surrounded by legs
> and skirts and couldn't see an awful lot. But when my mother
> and father held me up so I could see Ellis Island when we got to
> New York Harbor, I thought it was Aunt Emma's house. We then
> sat in the corner of a big room, my mother and I, while my father
> was doing paperwork. And at right angles to us was another
> mother and three children, all in very colorful costumes, with
> babushkas and scarves on their heads. And they were dancing. I
> stood with my mouth wide open. I'd never seen anything like
> this. And my mother took out the tin of Huntley & Palmers' bis-
> cuits and told me to offer some to these children. I went over and
> held out this tin box, and they looked at their mother. Their mother
> said something, and with that they each took one, and they smiled
> and I smiled. The next thing we were just jigging around together.
> We had no idea what the other one was saying, but we smiled
> and shared cookies, and it was a very happy situation.
>
> And then my father came for us, and again I was down
> among all the legs and skirts. We were just shuffling along
> through a doorway, and on each side there was a steel mesh
> type of fence. And suddenly this head popped up, and it was
> my aunt Emma, yelling, "Katie, Katie, Katie!" She was married
> to my mother's brother Jack, our sponsor. And then we went on
> a train to Newark, New Jersey—to my aunt's house. The thing
> I liked best was that it had a back porch with stairs that you

could go down, the back way in the open. There was a lot of activity on the street, a lot of carts and horses, and one day they had a merry-go-round. It came on a wagon. And I remember riding on the little wooden horses, and I thought, This is a wonderful country, with all these things you can do.

And then eventually we got our own place, which was two rooms in an attic. One room was the kitchen, living room, and dining room; the other was a bedroom with a cot for me. It was there where we had our first Christmas in America. I woke up in the morning and there was a little tree. It must have been all of twelve inches high. I've never had a tree that made an impression on me like that one did because I didn't expect it.

I had a bed of my own, and I could step outside on the roof to play. And there were two teenage boys downstairs, and they used to drive me all around on the back of their motorcycle. They would take me to the local candy store, sit me up on the counter, and give me all sorts of things to sing. I used to sing all the war songs, and they would give me candy and lollipops. I sat up there singing my heart out, and I made out like a bandit. It was a lark to them because I sang with an English accent.

They sent me to kindergarten in Newark for a while. We sat in a circle, and I had no idea what the kids were doing when they would get up or leave the room. I had to go and didn't know how to go about it. So they sent me home because I wet my pants, and my mother was mortified. I was supposed to raise my hand and ask to leave, but nobody had told me.

We eventually moved to Brooklyn, where my father was offered a job in a shoe factory, and I started school there when I was six, going on seven. The teachers thought my accent was wonderful and they put me in all the plays, but the kids fell on the floor laughing every time I spoke. I attended eight different grammar schools, because we moved a lot.

My mother was sort of overwhelmed by the moves. She thought there wouldn't be any trees, only cement, and that there wouldn't be gardens or flowers. She was relieved to find that there were some trees here. The tenement that we moved to had six families, three on each side. There was a Scottish lady on the top floor; we were very close to her. She was like the grandmother we didn't have here. And on the other side there were Italian and Polish families; we had a regular League of Nations. And when you went down the hall you could smell everything from kielbasa to corned beef and cabbage.

My mother never lost her love for the English way of life. We kept it, more or less. We had English Christmases and baked Yorkshire puddings—I grew up with that. My father applied for his citizenship papers immediately, and I became a citizen on his papers five years after he came. But my mother had to go and get her own papers, which took her a long time.

Eventually my parents bought their own home in Flatbush. And I went to Queens, where I was married and raised my two children. I ended up working for the payroll department of a state hospital. After I retired, I was running a senior center, and I still do a lot of volunteer work. I can look back and say I had a very productive life. I have wonderful children and grandchildren, a pension, Social Security, and a medical plan. I can do pretty much what I want to do, and nobody stops me. I still get excited when the sun comes up!

ELEANOR RUTH KENDERLINE LENHART emigrated with her parents from London in 1921, the year Congress passed the first federal immigration law to reduce mass migration to the United States.[4] The National-Origins Quota Act of 1921 restricted the admission of new immigrants to 3 percent of the number of persons of their nationality already living in the United States in 1910. The bulk of the admissible aliens under this law were northern and western Europeans. Eleanor was seven years old when she sailed on the *Berengeria* from Southampton to New York. She remembers:

Because of the war years, it was very difficult for my parents. My mother had six brothers and a married sister, and all the men went to World War I. So my mother and my aunt were left with their children and had to make do as best they could. Not far from us, in London, the zeppelins came over. As soon as the air raids came, they would put us babies on a mattress underneath a table with a drop leaf that went to the floor because that would protect us from the shrapnel that might fly through the window.

My father did not get back from the war until 1919. He had

a trade; he was a printer. He tried to go into business for himself but couldn't make a go of it. One of his brothers was a Methodist minister in Winona, Minnesota, and he wrote and said, "Do come to America. There'll be greater opportunities for you." He offered to be our sponsor, so my parents signed up for third-class passage on the *Berengeria.*

When we arrived on the boat my father was put in a cabin with three other men. My mother and I were put in with a British colonel's wife and her little boy. It turned out that the little boy had lice, and he had to be treated all the way over. My mother was absolutely horrified about the situation, but there wasn't a thing she could do about it. The day before we landed in New York, we were told to go to a stairway and line up: men, women, and children. There were doctors at the top of the stairway, and we were told to strip to the waist—everybody. My mother wouldn't hear of it. She said, "We'll just go to the end of the line," and we did. And when we got up to the doctors, mother said, "If you wish to examine us, you may come to our cabin." So we went back to our cabin, and nobody ever came, so we weren't examined.

When we got to New York Harbor, the first and second class passengers were allowed to just walk off, and the third class was quarantined for two days in the harbor and then sent to Ellis Island. When we were put on the barge, we were jammed in so tight that I couldn't turn around, and the stench was terrible. When we got to Ellis Island, they put the gangplank down, and there was a man shouting at the top of his voice, "Put your luggage here. Men this way; women and children this way." And Dad looked at us and said, "We'll meet you back there at this mound of luggage and hope we find it again. See you later."

So we went to this building where there were two women doctors standing at the door, with sticks in their hands, and they grabbed you and rolled your eyelids up on the sticks, looking for this infectious disease. Then we were sent to the building where the pews were, with desks all along the front. When it was our turn, my father (who had rejoined us) answered all of the questions. And the man said, "OK, you go through the door in back of me here. You are going into the United States."

We went through the door and found ourselves in a tun-

nel, and we came across a room that said YMCA—GUIDE. And
Dad said, "That's what we want. We need a guide to help us
get over to the mainland." And so he went inside, asked for a
guide, and a man came up to him grinning all over. He turned
out to be so helpful. He got our crates forwarded to Minnesota
and then got us to Grand Central Station. He found out that
there was just one train leaving for Minnesota, and that was
jammed full. We were two days late by then because we had
been quarantined two days in the New York Harbor. All that
was left on the train going to Winona was one upper berth, and
Dad said, "All right. I'll take the coach seat, and Mother and
daughter will use the upper berth."

It took a couple of days to get to Minnesota on the train,
and my parents knew nothing about dining cars. So my mother
said, "Well, we've got to eat." And she bought a carton of bread
and butter and cheese, and people were very kind to her about
explaining the [American] money and were very honest about
it. And then we got on the train.

That evening we met the porter, and of course I had never
seen a black man before. He was great, and he helped us up the
ladder to our berth. Then he took the ladder away, and we sat
there all night, we never undressed, and Mother said, "Eleanor,
America must be a very religious country. Every time we get to
a town the church bells are ringing." Of course, later on we
found out that was the train bell.

It must have been a very tense time for Mother. We spent
about a month in the parsonage in Winona before we got an
apartment of our own. I remember the food was so different,
especially breakfast. We always had eggs and bacon in England,
and they had cereal. I'd come home from school so hungry, and
Mother sneaked boxes of crackers and cookies up to our room,
so we wouldn't hurt anybody's feelings.

My father eventually took a job in Mount Morris, Illinois,
with a very large printing company, and the owners were very
kind to us. My parents never expressed any regret or remorse.
They were very happy in their place in Ogle County, Illinois. It
was seven miles from the county seat, and they walked seven
miles and back to get their citizenship papers. At the time they
took out their papers, I was still a minor, only thirteen years

old, and my name just appeared on their papers. I had no papers of my own.

When the Second World War came along, my parents were living in Florida, and I was doing a lot of volunteer work in different departments (in Washington, D.C.) for the war. I needed to be fingerprinted, and I had to prove I was a U.S. citizen. So I wrote my mother and asked her if she could send me the papers with my name on it, and she wrote, "I will not." She was worried they might get bent in the mail. So I went to the State Department and got my own papers.

In 1923, an Irish lass from County Limerick began her journey to America, traveling in steerage on the *Adriatic*. This is JOHANNA FLAHERTY's story.[5]

I was about seven years of age when I started school and continued school to the seventh grade. After the seventh grade there was really nothing in Ireland for me. I wasn't educated enough to take an office job, and my father could not afford to send me to business school or to college. . . . Then, in 1920, my aunt was here, and she said to me, "What are you going to do here? There's no job for you. Why don't you come to America with Uncle Patty? I'll send you to school and you'll get a job over there, and you can help your parents." So, in 1923, my uncle and I started out for this country. . . . I brought my clothes. That was about all.

The trip [from Queenstown to New York] wasn't bad, but we were down in steerage. That's the bottom of the boat. We had bunk beds, and the food was pretty good. But I was seasick most of the way across. And I didn't care if I ever saw food, just a glass of ginger ale. That was all I really wanted. Then I'd go upstairs and lie down on the deck, roll my coat up and put it under my head, and sleep there half the day. The sea was like glass at that time.

We landed down at the dock [in Manhattan] on a Friday evening. By Saturday morning they took us, by tender, to Ellis Island. Then we got a good look at the Statue of Liberty. We all went into Ellis Island, and we were lined up and we had to go up [into the Registry Room]. They had cages there, like you would see in a bank, and there was somebody behind each window. My uncle and I went up together. The inspector looked at his papers and said, "You can go." He looked at my papers and said, "Oh, you can't go." I said, "Why?" He said, "Well, you are not eighteen. You are a minor. Somebody will have to pick you up and sign for you." "Oh," I said, "my aunt told me she will be here." So he said, "Would you know your aunt?" I said, "Yes." So he said, "All right. Go back over there and sit down." So then we had to go back to these long benches and sit. There were maybe fifty to a hundred people sitting there. There were lots of women. They had their children with them—babies and younger children running around—all chattering away in their own language, and I didn't understand them. So after a while [the inspector] saw that I was kind of down in the dumps, and he called me and he said, "If your aunt came to the window now, would you know who she is?" I said, "There she is right behind you." She was standing at the side of the window. So he said, "All right, you can go with her."

We got on the El [train], and I saw everybody on the train was chewing. I couldn't imagine how come everybody was chewing and nobody was putting food in their mouths. A few days later I learned that it was chewing gum. . . . The city was kind of terrifying, those large buildings. It seemed like they were just about to close in on you. But I got used to it very fast.

I went to Merchants & Bankers' Business School for a year, and then I graduated. After I graduated I got a job with the Metropolitan Life Insurance Company and worked there for thirteen years. Then I married, had three children, and I didn't go back to work until my last child was in high school. I went to work for Spotless Dry Cleaners and became a manager for one of their stores. And I went from there to St. Barnabas Hospital and worked there as a ward clerk for about fourteen years. I retired from there when I was seventy-two.

I never was sorry that I left Ireland. . . . I love it, over there, for a vacation, but I wouldn't want to stay. I was here a week, and I went down to the Naturalization Office to see if I could become a citizen. He asked, "How old are you?" I said, "I'll be seventeen in a couple of weeks." So he said, "Come back to us after you are eighteen."

I met my husband in New York. Our families knew each other at home, but we never met in Ireland. We lived in the Bronx for about thirty years. We belonged to Our Savior Parish. The kids were all brought up in Our Savior School, and they went to Catholic high school after that. They are all married now and have their own children. One son is about to become a lawyer, the other is a computer analyst, and my daughter Mary works for Edison. I am mighty glad I came here. God bless America, is all I can say.

DONALD ROBERTS left Wales as a twelve-year-old in the spring of 1925. Together with his parents, a younger brother, and two younger sisters, he sailed on the *Aquitania*.[6]

I was born in a mining village in Wales in 1913. The First World War was about to erupt. The war took a terrible toll in Britain, because there was such a slaughter of men. After the war was over, my father, who had been a captain in the Army, decided that he should try to come to America to better the lot of the family.

We were put on a quota list. My father was in this country for almost four years. Then he came back. Our names finally came up, and my parents sold the house and furniture and packed some things in wooden boxes, and off we sent to Southampton. We left in the latter part of April. Our ship was very crowded. We picked up in Cherbourg a lot of people from southern and central Europe—our first contact with "foreigners." My feelings about leaving were mixed.

We had a small cabin for the six of us, and we managed pretty good. We were in the third-class passage, and we used to go out on the afterdeck of the vessel for air. People were lying around any place they could find to stay out in the open air rather than get back to the stifling conditions inside the ship.

I will always remember a horse that was being carried over from Europe. His name was Tony, and he belonged to Tom Mix, the movie star. They used to bring the horse out on the deck for a little exercise, and some of us kids had our pictures taken on Tony's back.

We arrived in New York in early May, and the ships at this

time used to stop at quarantine in the outer harbor, before you came into the Narrows. All the incoming ships used to put up the quarantine flag, the yellow flag, until the ship was cleared to come into the inner harbor. People all lined up for a medical examination. But the result of that examination required us to be detained in Ellis Island. My mother was taken away and isolated in a hospital area because she was suspected of having tuberculosis.

My father and us four kids were kept in a separate area and given a small little room with a few bunks. The place smelled of disinfectants, like a hospital. There was a man who came around every morning and every afternoon, with a stainless steel cart, like the Good Humor man. He was dressed in white, and he would blow a whistle or ring a bell, and all the kids would line up. He had small paper cups, and every kid got a little warm milk.

They would also blow a whistle or ring a gong when it was time for meals. We would walk down seemingly endless corridors, all with white tiles on the sides, down and around. And finally we came to a big hall with long wooden tables and benches. And the waiters would come out and put the food on the table.

I can especially remember the breakfasts. The breakfasts were invariably eggs. The eggs were cooked in big wire baskets, and they would put the wire baskets out and set them on the table. And these southern Europeans would be grabbing these eggs and breaking them open and egg yolk would be running down their faces, and they would take bread almost from under your nose and snatch the stuff away from you. That was the sum and substance of the table etiquette. Not that we went hungry!

During the days that we were waiting, we would be let out in the morning and the afternoon for an hour or so to get some exercise in the yard. The yard had a wire fence about fifteen feet high. And once in a while we could see my mother at the window of the hospital, waving to us kids and my father. We could see everything going on in the harbor, and the Statue of Liberty was very close.

The days went by, and ultimately my mother was released.

She had no TB, but she had suffered from bronchitis. The day, two weeks after our arrival in Ellis Island, when we were allowed to come into the country, that was a real banner day. We got a ferryboat that ran back and forth from Ellis Island to the Battery. And we just walked off, like birds let out of the cage.

We had several advantages in entering the country. We had no language barrier, and my father, having worked in New York and lived on Staten Island for three or four years, was familiar with the area. So we went up to Twenty-third Street to the Cornish Arms Hotel. It was a place where the British went. And I, being the oldest, had to ride herd on the other kids while my parents went to look for a place to live.

They went by ferry across to Jersey City, got on a train, and got off at the first stop, Rutherford. Across the street from the train station was a real estate agent who took them for a ride down the street. After living at the hotel for about a week, we moved into a house in Rutherford without a stick of furniture. A couple of neighbor ladies came in and offered us some tea, and my parents went to the hardware store to buy some cups and saucers. We slept on the floor that night, strangers in a strange land.

We were dressed like British kids with short pants, rosy cheeks, and we must have stood out like a sore thumb. It didn't take long, a few weeks, before kids used to gang up on us and try to beat us up. Many a time we used to run home and just make it home before this gang of kids would catch us. But my father, as a young man, had been a boxer. He was handy with his fists. So he bought my brother and me a set of boxing gloves, and he said, "I am gonna teach you how to defend yourself because you are not gonna be running home every day." After a while, we gave as much as we got, and after a while we were left alone. But to compound that, the first year we were here, this place was alive with mosquitoes. We had very bad screens in the house, so for one whole season we had to contend with all their bites and we all broke out in blisters. That was our initiation to America.

Now we weren't here very long before the Great Depression set in. And my father, being in the building line, found himself out of work, as did millions of other people. We had saved some money, and we were very frugal with our savings. My father was too proud to ask for any relief. A day came when there was no money and very little food in the house. But a wonderful thing happened. When I came home for lunch that day, a hundred-dollar check had come from my mother's brother, who was an engineer with the Twenty Mule Team Borax Company in Death Valley, California.

But then my father couldn't make the mortgage payments, so he asked the loan company if they would allow him just to pay the interest. And in exchange for that he would do repair on the houses they were foreclosing. The arrangement was made. My parents had to come up with twenty-five dollars a month to pay the interest, and they kept the house. And then my father was able to get a job through the Work Projects Administration (WPA) that was started by President [Franklin Delano] Roosevelt [FDR].

A few years ago, my wife and I took one of our grandchildren over to the Statue of Liberty. There was a museum there that depicted the history of immigration, broken down by nationality. Being Welsh, I was interested in seeing something about the Welsh coming to this country. Welsh people arrived early in America. They came over to work in the coal mines in Pennsylvania and the slate quarries and the marble quarries in Vermont and New Hampshire. And many of the leaders in the War of Independence were Welsh people. The man who financed the Revolution was a Welshman.

But I saw nothing about this in the exhibit. So I contacted some influential people of Welsh origin, and as a result there is an ongoing program now to recognize their contributions. And on another visit to Ellis Island, the guide invited anybody who might have passed through Ellis Island to come forward and speak, and I spoke to them.

I am glad if I can contribute in a small way to your compilations of the history of Ellis Island and recording for future generation the contributions of Welsh people to this country.

ANNE REILLY QUINN emigrated from Paisley, Scotland (near Glasgow) in 1928, at the age of nine.[7] She sailed with her father, mother, and older brother from Southampton on a German ship that had served as a troopship in World War I. This trip was the *Leviathan*'s last as a passenger ship, and while crossing the Atlantic, a tidal wave inundated the four-bunk cabin in which Annie's family slept. After a day's delay, the ship arrived in New York on Easter Sunday, and the Reillys were ferried to Ellis Island, where they were held overnight.

We were held over because my father had suffered a stroke due to injuries he had received in the First World War. He lost the power of speech and one of his arms was paralyzed. He could walk and he could hear, but the inspectors were afraid he would become a burden to the state. But fortunately the doctor found him fit and well the next day, and we were released into the custody of my eldest brother, who had come to the United States six years previously.

I remember that boys went with the men and girls went with the women during inspection. But my mother absolutely refused to part with my younger brother. He was only seven and had been very ill, and she said, "Where I go, he goes." And he was allowed to go with us to the women's quarters, which were very, very clean.

But at breakfast the next morning, my mother only drank tea; she wouldn't eat her oatmeal. And across from us sat a Turkish man who wore a fez and looked hungry. And when he realized we weren't eating the oatmeal he said, "No eat?" And my mother said "No. . . . You want this?" And he said, "Me eat, me eat," and my mother passed all the bowls to him and he ate everything. That poor man was starving.

We caught the last ferry that afternoon from Ellis Island to New York. Most of our hand luggage had been lost in the tidal wave, but we had a steamer trunk with some heirlooms in it. We first moved to Harrison and then to Kearney, which was the target of a lot of Scottish immigrants at the time because there were mills in Kearney that were actually part of the mills in Scotland. And there were a lot of Irish immigrants in this town also. In Scotland, because of our name, we were considered Irish, and we were Roman Catholic, which was another plot against us in Protestant Scotland, so my mother never regretted coming to the United States. And I fit right in after people stopped teasing me because of my accent.

We didn't have any electricity in Scotland, and here you flick on a switch and the light comes on. And there were so many cars here compared to the town we came from, and we didn't have the large tall buildings that New York has. But my mother, on a visit to Kansas, where her brother lived, was quite taken aback to see signs in bus depots announcing that "No Colored Will Be Served." It astounded her that this could happen in this country that she loved with all her heart.

Our way of life at home was just the same as it had been. My mother did a lot of the type of cooking that she did when we lived in Scotland, and our chief entertainment was singing and the Scottish highland dances that we learned in the Catholic high school in Kearney. I graduated from there toward the end of the Depression, and first worked in a laundry and then did office work in a linen thread mill. I married in 1943, and we have raised seven children and eight grandchildren.

I have enjoyed my life. We've had a very happy life.

3

From the Pale of Settlement to the Golden Land

At the beginning of the twentieth century, some 4.9 million Jews lived in the "Pale of Settlement," those twenty-five provinces that extended from Lithuania on the Baltic Sea, through Byelorussia and the Ukraine, to Odessa on the Black Sea. Czarist edicts confined the Jews to densely populated villages, or "shtetls," surrounded by a sea of Russians. Numerous attacks on Jewish communities called "pogroms" led to organized massacres and looting of Jewish property.

Life became increasingly more intolerable for the Jewish minority. Jews were systematically discriminated against in higher education and in economic affairs. Famines, epidemics, and the onset of World War I contributed to a massive exodus of Russian and Polish Jews, with some two million immigrating to the United States between 1899 and 1931.

The Hebrew Immigrant Aid Society (HIAS) was one of the leading service agencies to offer support to immigrants at Ellis Island. The society's foremost task was to assist and comfort Jewish immigrants, particularly orphaned children who arrived without a family and persons who were detained. HIAS representatives helped Jewish aliens file appeals against exclusion and deportation. During the 1930s and 1940s, they also assisted Jewish refugees who wanted to change their status from nonimmigrant visitors to permanent residents.[1]

* * *

SADIE GUTTMAN KAPLAN worked for the HIAS for seventeen years in its Manhattan headquarters and in an office on Ellis Island. Born near Odessa, she was twelve years old when her family came to New York in 1905, because her older brothers were about to be drafted in the Russian army. She graduated at age sixteen from business school in Brooklyn, and the HIAS hired her as a secretary because she knew how to type and was fluent in three languages: English, Russian, and Yiddish.[2]

> Our work was with the immigrants who came here who didn't have anybody to take care of them, and some of the officials wanted to send them back. Our job was to intervene and take responsibility for them. We used to take the immigrants to our building on East Broadway, to shelter them and feed them, and to try and locate some jobs for them. People used to come in, crying and crying. They all had their share of heartache, and you tried to do the best you could for them.
>
> My boss asked me if I would like to go to our office on Ellis Island to work there for a while, and so I went. It was like bedlam there. Every day we had immigrants who didn't have anybody [to sponsor them] come into our office. We had to register them and make up their affidavits, if they needed them. Having been an immigrant myself, I knew what they were going through. I tried to be considerate and have sympathy for them.
>
> We had to be on the ferryboat every morning by eight thirty. It took us half an hour to get over to the island. We used to say "Good Morning" to the Statue of Liberty every day. A couple of years ago, we went for an evening out for dinner on the boat, and I got such a kick when I saw the statue right near me because my grandson said, "Grandma, all your life you saw her!"

IRVING HALPERIN was born in a small shtetl near Minsk and remembers a "very comfortable" childhood. He was five years old when he immigrated with his mother and a younger brother to the

United States in 1909. His father, a carpenter, had arrived a year earlier.[3]

> The main reason we left was to have more freedom and a better economic life. In Russia, no matter how good things were, there was always the cloud over you that something might explode. You always had that fear. I remember sneaking across the border at night. That was a custom then. They had to pay the guide. We finally wound up in Antwerp, where we got on the boat *Veendam,* and we were in steerage.
>
> The food was terrible. You had all kinds of smells—herring and salami—and stuff like that was all over the place. I remember being all over the ship—I used to run around up on deck—and watch the dolphins jumping in the water. I remember going to Ellis Island, through the fenced-off section. It didn't take us too long because my father was waiting for us there; he had made all the arrangements and picked us up.
>
> We went right over to Bayonne, New Jersey, and we lived there and I went to school there. I enjoyed school very much. That's the wonderful thing! There were so many immigrant children there, and somehow you absorb the language, running around and playing with them and with the children who were already born here.
>
> I was an omnivorous reader. I read all the time, every book in the public library. I used to enjoy reading historical novels. I knew so much history, I used to drive the teachers crazy in school. I had one teacher who wanted to get rid of me, so she skipped me a grade. Then she was put in charge of my next class. She skipped me again.
>
> I got out of high school at sixteen and got a job in the post office as a railway mail clerk. They sent me to Philadelphia, and then I got a transfer to the Pennsylvania terminal in New York, to be closer to my family. I was supposedly eighteen. My father had made a mistake on my citizen papers and made me two years older. That was the only proof I had. I had no birth certificate. I worked about two years there.
>
> Then I went to work for my father, who had become a builder. I joined the union, and when I was twenty-three years old, I registered at New York University downtown because I

wanted to go to college. I went five nights a week, four hours a night, for four years and got a degree in accounting and commercial science. We call it "business administration" today.

During the Depression I worked as a carpenter for the WPA. We only worked so many hours, but we got union wages. Then I took a civil service job and went to work for the state of New Jersey's Unemployment Insurance Office. I began there for about thirty-five dollars a week; when I finished I had doubled my salary.

SALLY (SURKA) KLEINMAN GURIAN was eight years old when she came with her mother and younger sister to the United States. She was born in a small town near Odessa. Her father was a blacksmith, and his competitor burned their house down one night while the family was asleep. The local priest took them in, and her mother, in gratitude, would bake challah and strudels for him on Jewish holidays. Her family got along well with the Gentiles in town, but the Russian government issued increasingly more restrictive edicts.[4]

If we had to move from one place to another, we had to report to the government. They didn't allow you to move wherever you wanted to. And after our house burned down, we were very frightened. My mother's brother came to America first and sent for my father and got him started on a job as an ironworker. A year and a half later, in 1914, we came over on the maiden voyage of the German ship *Vaterland,* which was later captured by the Americans in World War I and renamed *Leviathan.*

We took a few clothes, some bedding, and silverware, just bundles. We went steerage, but everything was nice and new. Everybody thought that when you got to America, there would be gold on the floor for you to pick up. When we got to New York Harbor and saw the Statue of Liberty, everybody cheered. And as we got off, all the children got little American flags and little boxes of candy.

I remember my father coming with my aunt. And we didn't recognize my father at first, because he had a beard when he was in Europe, and now he was clean shaven. And my aunt bought us ice cream, but we weren't used to ice cream. It was too cold. We immediately went to Brooklyn, where we stayed with my uncle's stepsister until we found an apartment in Williamsburg.

We didn't know any English, and in school we sat in a large class with a lot of immigrant children. You know how cruel children can be. They called us "Greenhorn" and "Popcorn" and all these names. So we studied real hard. We managed very well, and we loved school. We had very good teachers, and they were very patient with us. By the time I got to seventh grade, there was a terrible flu, and a lot of the teachers were out sick. I had a wonderful principal, Miss Olson, and she called me in and said to me, "Sally, how would you like to teach a second grade class, because we are short of teachers?" And I did, and I loved it. The children were just wonderful.

When I finally graduated, I worked in the Home Pattern Company in Brooklyn. A girl I worked with got a job with the Metropolitan Life Company and encouraged me to apply. I had to put my religion down on the application, and one of the managers said, "Sorry, but we can't hire any Jewish girls." But I got the job anyway. I think I was the first Jewish girl working for the Metropolitan Life Insurance Company. And when I had worked there for a year, my manager asked me if I knew anybody else who would like a job at Metropolitan, and I said, "Well I have a cousin, but, of course, she is Jewish." And that same manager said, "Well, it really doesn't matter if she is a good worker. We'll be glad to hire her."

I worked for Metropolitan Life for twenty-five years. They gave me continuous employment until I retired when I was in my fifties. When I got my job with Metropolitan I had two witnesses who went with me from the office, and I got my naturalization papers. They were right there with me when the judge said, "You are a naturalized citizen," and my two witnesses had to sign. It was very thrilling.

CELIA ADLER came as a twelve-year-old alone to the United States to join two older sisters. Grieving for her parents, who had stayed behind, she left her small town at the Russian-Polish border in 1914 in the company of a family that "adopted" her for the journey's duration.[5]

They just between the two of them had made up their mind for me to go. I got upset because I loved my parents, and I loved my home, and I loved my friends. But my sisters sent the ticket for the ship's passage, and my mother, who was afraid that maybe I wouldn't have enough food, baked a bag full of "zaharas" to take along. You cut a slice of bread, and you dip it in vinegar and sugar, and you bake it, and it keeps for God knows how long. And I had a new hat and new dress and a basket to put the bag of zaharas in.

The whole town came out to say good-bye. And before I got in the wagon [for the overland journey] my father took me to the rabbi. He stood up and put both hands on my head and blessed me. That's one time I wanted to cry. Then the driver came into the house and said, "Let's go." And that's when the couple who took me on as their "adopted" child came with their own daughter. Somebody picked me up and put me in the wagon. I was crying because all of a sudden I was not near my real mother any more.

From the border to Warsaw we went on the train, and then we had to go through the length of Warsaw to take another train to Antwerp. I was fascinated by the noises the train made. When we got to Antwerp and checked into a hotel, we found out that there were no ships going to America anymore. We stayed in the hotel for a week.

My new mother made me very comfortable, and the little girl was helpful, too. A lady from the hotel had a daughter my age, and they took me for an outing to a large park, and I sort of snapped out of my fear and depression. All of a sudden the proprietor of the hotel came in and said, "I want you to know that a ship is here, and it might be the last ship to America. Do you want to go, or do you want to go back home?" I just went on board the ship and came, and here I am.

We were on the ship for about four weeks, and they were very bad days. We were taken all the way down to steerage. You didn't have any light down there. Most people were sea-sick. We had mattresses on the floor and on the sides. There were people all over. We slept in our clothes, and everybody had their baggage. I just had a small basket with all my belong-ings. I had the zaharas and an extra skirt and blouse. When the ship finally stopped, it was very early in the morning. One little boy used to sneak up from third class to the deck to see what was happening. He was the first one to see the lights of America, and he came running down screaming, "I see America! The lights are burning!" By the time I got up, I saw a strip of light as far as the eyes could see. Everybody grabbed their clothes, their baggage, and all kinds of bags.

Before I knew what happened I was standing by the rail and the whole world was lit. And I saw the Statue of Liberty. When we were talking about it in steerage, I learned that the Statue of Liberty gives you freedom and everybody the right to form an opinion of their own.

Then a ferry came and took us to Ellis Island. There were lots of doctors; they checked your eyes and throat. When the inspectors came to me, they wouldn't let me go with my sister because she had no way of showing how she would support me.

So I had to stay overnight. The family I traveled with was gone. They had a brother who took them, and we just said good-bye and they were gone. I didn't know what was going to happen to me. It got dark. We were rushed into a big building, and hundreds of people were given a bowl of soup and a wooden spoon, and I still had my zaharas to eat. From the dining room we went into an even bigger room where they had hammocks. A man came by and pulled me up, and I remained sitting on the hammock all night. I didn't sleep a wink.

At daylight I jumped down from the hammock, still with my hat and hatpins on. I reached the floor and walked. They started to call us, in many languages, and asked us to stand in line. Then I saw my older sister on the other side of the gate, with her little three-year-old girl. She had the proper identification papers with her. I didn't know my sister—she had left before I was born—but I recognized her from the pictures she sent.

We walked out of Ellis Island together to the docks, took a ferry, and then a trolley to Bayonne, New Jersey. My sister had been in this country for quite a few years, and all of a sudden, here I am—the Greenhorn. I had held onto my basket and to my hat that was pinned up, and she was sure that anyone who would see me would know that I had just got off the boat. And she didn't want that. She made me take everything out, wrapped it in paper, and put it under my arm. Then she left my basket with my hat behind on Ellis Island. I looked back until I didn't see it anymore. It was my whole treasure. I didn't dare say anything to my sister. She could turn me around and send me back!

I stayed with my sister in Bayonne for several weeks until a cousin in New York got me a job with a dressmaker at four dollars a week. In the first few years I spoke only Yiddish with my sisters. Then I learned English in night school, but they still considered me a Greenhorn.

By that time I lived in an apartment with four people who had lost their parents. The youngest of the four was a schoolboy. The oldest sister, who ran the household, told him, "You will have to take Tzpky (Celia) to the dressmaker when you go to school in the morning." But he didn't want to walk with me because everybody saw I was a Greenhorn.

He said to me, "If you see my friends, go behind me. Don't go straight." Until one day I said to myself, "I am going to make a mark somewhere else," and I noticed that at the corner where we turned there was a wine store with Jewish initials. The next day I told him, "I am not going with you." So the older sister came running, "You'll get lost. We won't be able to find you." But I didn't listen. I walked out with my nose up, and I got to that store with the Jewish sign. I turned, and I got to my dressmaker.

Through the years I helped my parents with whatever I could, but I also managed to save a little money, and I went to the mountains every summer. The dressmaker had one worker, a little bit older than I, and she took me downtown to East Broadway. And I met people in night school—an English girl who spoke Yiddish—and I read an awful lot.

I visited museums and places, and I knew U.S. history quite well before I got my citizen papers. That was an exciting day. My sister and my nephew were my witnesses.

I wasn't married until I was twenty-eight years old, and then I raised a son. He went five years through Hebrew school and four years in high school. He received a medal for science and a certificate of honor every year. Then he went to Brooklyn College and graduated cum laude. After two years in the army, he went to New York University to get his master's degree and received a grant to spend a year at the Sorbonne. Now he is a city planner and has given me two beautiful grandchildren, twins. I am very proud of him.

I am very happy to be here. This country stands for a lot of things. It gives you a lot of freedom—a happier life to live than under the czar, for sure. I missed my parents but I didn't miss my hometown, because as I got older, I realized that there wasn't a life for young people there. I was glad that I got help, and they took me away.

KATE SIMON was four years old in 1918 when she traveled with her mother and two-year-old brother across a war-ravaged Europe from Warsaw to Rotterdam, their point of departure for America. They were carrying their belongings in a bundle, a huge bedcover, the foremost treasure of a Jewish family from a cold country. Her father had left for the United States two years earlier. Aboard the ship in steerage, typhus, a disease carried by lice, was rampant. When they arrived at Ellis Island, Kate remembers the terror.[6]

Would we be excluded because of my brother's rickets? I remember clinging to my mother and meeting my father, who looked like a God to me. He, whose existence I had doubted, was absolutely gorgeous, and he had a sweet mouth. He had been munching on chocolate while he was waiting for us. After that we went to stay with my father's uncle, who had two impaired daughters—one very lively but practically blind, the other one a deaf-mute, silent, remote. We didn't understand each other, because their Polish had deteriorated.

But then we moved and took in boarders. My father, despite his Olympic looks, had a Prussian attitude toward us: "You've got to do what I say, whether it makes sense or not." I was growing angry with him and stayed angry when he left us. But I remember with great pleasure when we lived on East Ninety-eighth Street. There were small houses in which there were black kids joyously running up and down the porches, gathering under religious banners, marching up and down the street, and singing—a very happy thing to watch and listen. This was the better part of America.

And then we moved to the fresh air and the new schools in the Bronx. My mother went back to work when we entered school. She was a very independent person with an extraordinary intelligence that never had an opportunity to develop. My mother had visions of my going to school and didn't think it was important whether I got married or not.

I learned English very rapidly in school because I wanted to, and I was very careful to imitate what I thought was the best-sounding English. That came from the librarians and going to the library classes. The public libraries gave classes in English! Almost instantly, as soon as we went to school, my mother established herself in these classes. That was her Americanization. And we had the advantage of living in a mixed neighborhood. The mix was largely Italian and Jewish and everything else but black and Chinese.

The phrase "becoming Americanized" never occurred to me. I was too busy living, too busy learning everything: habits, languages, people, places, finding out in a thousand different ways who you are. I knew I spoke English well, quite early, and I knew I wrote well quite early. But the learning and the enlightenment, I felt I could have gotten that in any language, had I wanted to.

The only situation in which I felt very strongly that there was a "them" and "I" was that in those days when you applied for a job, you had to put down a religion. Now we were not religious, but I was damned if I was not going to put down Jewish, if I was asked, and not Protestant or Catholic. That was my only sense of not being Americanized, in that I was not part of a majority. The Borough Hall also had the quality of "them." If we ever had to be taken to Borough Hall, we were in trouble—citizenship trouble—and with the cops, something terrible.

We lived in a very neat and lively tenement area, very well kept by janitors who were Polish. There were lively Romanian and Hungarian ladies who were not as devoted, the other ladies said, as the Russians and Italians. The Italian mothers were the most devoted. They were like warm stoves. The Italian kids used to have wine for lunch and sleep through the afternoon. And I thought they were wonderful. I was envious of this pagan life. The Jewish mothers were more interested in their children's achievement.

One of my memories that's very vivid is that I used to like to get up very early in the morning and watch the street wake up, my street. All those people belonged to me. There was the Third Avenue El, and on one corner there was the candy store where we bought ice cream on Friday night. And at another corner there was my tree, one tree that had white blossoms. There was a small synagogue on the next street. Two blocks up, there was the Belmont Movie House, where you went every Saturday at one o'clock, and there was always some adult who would buy you a ticket. And then, of course, there was the best place of all, which was the library. It was a great adventure. We would take out two books, and the librarians were terribly nice. The idea that there were all these books, and they were mine, and I had the privilege of reading them, was very exciting.

And then there were schools from which you progressed to the sixth grade and then eighth grade, all within a few blocks. And then there was a wonderful Italian market. And I could not always tell the difference between the Jewish families and the Italian families. They all made the same noises, in different languages; they slapped their kids the same way; they caressed them the same way. There was the man who showed us dirty pictures, and there was a grocery store near the candy store where the boys used to steal potatoes and bake them in an empty lot.

And of course sleeping on a fire escape was an immigrant experience. I remember it as extraordinary, beautiful, dark, and all the white sheets and people sitting in little groups and talking quietly. The one thing that I think was a great advantage in our growing up, besides the fact that we had to learn to be stubborn and strong and willful to exist, was the street life. It was a very honorable society. There was a great deal of trust and interdependence. I think it's so sad that's almost altogether gone.

Nobody ever told us that we had to be happy. No one ever promised us that. "This is life," we learned. And it had to be lived. And you take what you can, and you endure what you have to endure. I think this may be true of many, many immigrants, whether they have expressed it or not. So many American children are brought up from the very first day with the sense that everything should be directed at making them happy. There is no recognition of the fact that you have to feel bad at times, and that's part of the feeling good at times. We had that, and when we felt good, we felt very good.

It was the time of the Depression, and there was no place to go but up! There wasn't the kind of lassitude that kids live through now. We were involved in everything, whether actively or in the sense of being emotionally tied to some idea. There was so much to learn. There were teachers who were very passionate about teaching to the point of giving you extra time. I was very greedy so I took as much as I could.

The Ellis Island experience and everything that went before it and came after was the beginning of making me a travel writer—the watching, the listening, the learning of phrases, the tremendous awareness at all times, and a certain kind of responsiveness to all people. That is part of the immigration thing, the sense of mingling with Americans that fosters curiosity rather than xenophobia.

HARRY SINGER (GIRSCHKOV ZINGERMAN) was twelve years old when he arrived in 1920 in the United States. He was born in a small town in the Ukraine, where he lived with his mother, two sisters, and three cousins in the house of his grandfather, who was the cantor in the local synagogue. He received a traditional, orthodox education from a rabbi who taught him the Hebrew alphabet and the Torah. His father had left for America when he was three years old. After World War I ended, the rest of the family set out for the United States.[7]

We had wagons. When we reached the Polish border, the border guards started shooting at us, but my uncle had some money with him, so he bought them off. And the following day we arrived in Poland and took the train to Warsaw. I was amazed that they could have trains going without being pulled by horses! From there (after we got a visa) we went to Germany, from Germany we went to Belgium, and from Belgium we took a boat to Liverpool. And from Liverpool we sailed on the *Acquitana* to Ellis Island.

It was a voyage of about two weeks, and we used to go on the deck to watch the whales. The crewmen would give us oranges and other kinds of fruit. I'd never tasted oranges before. When we came into New York Harbor, we saw the Statue of Liberty. Everybody was on deck and everybody was happy. We stayed at Ellis Island for about a day while they examined us, but all of us were well and they let us go. We took a little boat to New York and a train from New York to Boston. The guides put labels on us when we boarded the train to show that we were immigrants and couldn't speak any English, and people would help us get around.

The first day we came to Peabody, we met my father and I started school. There was a special class for immigrant children. It was a class for all immigrant children who couldn't speak English, and there was a special teacher—she was very good— who taught us how to speak English and write. And I picked it up in about two or three months, enough so I could enter the fifth grade. There were a lot of Greek children in my class and a few Polish children. Peabody was a town where they had a lot of leather factories, and all the immigrants, including my father, used to get jobs there. And my older sister worked in a "bleachery," where they used to bleach cloth, and helped my father support the family.

I stayed in school until I graduated from high school, but even while I went to school I used to work in a leather factory from about six o'clock a.m. to about eight in the morning. I did this until I graduated, and then I went to accounting school at night. I got a job in the payroll department at the A. C. Lawrence Leather Company—a big company—and I stayed with them for forty-six years.

My father had very little education, so he never became a citizen, but my mother attended night school and she became a citizen. They were both happy they had come to America and glad to be away from the Communist Revolution in Russia. Our social life in the United States centered around people who attended the same synagogue, and that's where I met my wife, at a dance at the YMHA [Young Men's Hebrew Association] in Lynn.

We have two daughters and a son and seven grandchildren. My son is finishing law school in England, and one of my daughters lives in Israel now and is married to a rabbi. I am very proud to be here in this country, and I thank God that I was able to make a nice living for my family and children.

With her mother and her nine-year-old brother, ROSE SIEGAL ALBER LEVINE came from Russia in 1921 when she was eleven years old. Her father had left in 1914 to escape the draft. During World War I, he did not correspond with his family. They lived in one room in a boarding house in Ruvno, and they were often hungry and cold. But the mother insisted that her children learn to read and write Hebrew and a few words of Russian.[8]

I had a playmate who was a richer kid than I. She and I went to the same rabbi, who taught us. She used to pay me to do her homework. She used to give me a piece of cake, challah, a penny. She loved me because I did her homework, and I got smarter.

After the war, my mother got a letter from my father with tickets for passage to America. We rode on a train to Warsaw—the HIAS was there—and she got a passport. And then we took a train to Antwerp, and we had to change trains in Belgium. My mother went into the train, the doors closed fast behind her, and my brother and I were left on the platform. We started screaming, but some adults took care of us and took us to the next stop, where my mother waited.

In Antwerp we walked out from the station and onto the boat. We were immigrants, and we were in third class. They didn't have much food, mostly herrings and water. All of the adults got sick, but none of the children did. We were running around, and we were having a lot of fun, playing cards. And we were on the boat during Hannukah, lighting candles every day.

I couldn't see the Statue of Liberty when we arrived because everybody was standing in front of me and I was a little kid. When we got to Ellis Island, my mother got through with all her papers, and then a man runs over and grabs her, and her hat fell off. I didn't know my father and my mother didn't know her husband, because he had had a beard in Europe and here he had shaved off his beard. We went on a barge and I asked,

"So where is America?" And then they took a taxi and went to the house where my dad lived. It was a railroad flat. I started walking and asked, "Where is the chair where you fly up?" I meant the elevator.

The next morning I said to my brother, "Come, come, let's look around America!" It was a few blocks down to the East River, but I was smart enough to make a sign. There was a barbershop with that thing that turns. I made a sign every time we passed one, and we found our way home. The neighborhood was all Jewish, and the school was on the next block. We registered there after the Christmas break.

I had a teacher who knew how to speak Jewish (Yiddish). Miss Critel in 1-A was very nice. She spoke to me in Jewish and explained to me what she was teaching. I was very anxious to learn, and I felt good because I was learning English. So I learned fast and got good marks. I loved school, and they kept skipping me. In five years, I made the whole eight years of school.

My parents were happy that they made the decision to come to America and to send me to school. When I graduated, I looked for a job. It was in January, a miserable day. I was cold. I saw a sign in downtown Manhattan on Greene Street, "Girl Wanted." It was an underwear place, Littman and Wolfson, and they said, "If you want to work, we'll put you to work." And I made twenty-seven dollars the first week! I worked about two years there.

Then the forelady was getting married, and I became the forelady. I worked for six years. Then I got married in 1933 and had a child, and then my first husband died. I went back to work for twelve years and raised my only child until I married Max Levine in 1955. I lived with him until he died in 1986.

Now, since I am alone, I joined the (senior) center, and I am a volunteer. I go every day to the center and serve lunches there, and I do arts and crafts. I had a full life. It wasn't always an easy life, but I love America. It's "My Country, 'Tis of Thee."

4

The Italian Bambini

The Italians represented the largest single group of immigrants who passed through Ellis Island. Some 3.3 million came from the south, from the central and southern part of the peninsula and from Sicily. Some 620,000 came from the north, from Piedmont, Lombardy, Tuscany, and the French, Austrian, and Swiss border regions.[1]

The average Italian family, living in the midst of great natural beauty, seldom had enough to eat. The small farms on the barren hillsides could not produce enough food to feed the extended families. People listened eagerly to the labor agents who visited Italy to recruit workers for American industries and read the letters of family members or neighbors who had traveled in steerage to try their luck in America.

At the end of their voyage many found only the humblest and most back-breaking jobs: digging ditches and sewers, pouring cement, and working in the iron and copper mines of the upper Midwest and the granite quarries of Maine. But in time they saved some money and started small businesses of their own.

Their children studied hard, and some went to college. They became lawyers, teachers, principals, and politicians. Edward Corsi, who came to the United States at age ten in 1907— when the largest number of Italian immigrants arrived at Ellis Island—was appointed Commissioner of Immigration and Naturalization for the New York District in 1931. Twenty-four years after he had passed through Ellis Island as a child immigrant, he returned there to take his oath of office.

"The ride across the harbor, with the Statue of Liberty looming high upon the left, brought back a thousand memories," he wrote in his autobiography. "I thought of that other day when we had come through—of my mother who had entered the country with high hope, but at last gone back to Italy in desperation to die.

"I enjoyed the crowds, and the good fellowship of the East Side. Down the street on which I lived there was a little brownstone house. . . . It was a settlement house. . . . The gang of boys with whom I played had decided to organize a club and have a baseball team. . . . We needed a clubroom, and mustering all our courage, we applied and were admitted on probation. . . . It was as if a wide door to America had been opened for me."[2]

After graduating from Fordham University with a law degree, Edward Corsi became director of Haarlem Settlement House and made it the center of neighborhood life. He opened playgrounds for children, clubs for mothers, and classes in English and citizenship. He helped thousands of immigrants who passed through its doors to become Americans.

"I congratulate you, Corsi," a friend said on the day after his appointment as Commissioner of Immigration and Naturalization at Ellis Island. "You've got one of the most important jobs in the country. You'll be helping to *make* America." And so he did.

* * *

ORESTE TEGLIA immigrated with his mother, two brothers, and two sisters to America when he was twelve years old. His father had left earlier to work on the railroad. For a decade his mother had supported her family in Tuscany by growing and selling grapes, peaches, pears, and figs and by raising chickens and pigs to sell in the local market. They had to wait two years for a visa that would allow them to join his father in the United States. They finally left in 1916, in the middle of World War I.[3]

> I was very sad to leave, mostly because of my dog, Pisarino. I
> left him in my bed, where he had slept with me. There was no

way to take him along. We went by train through a lot of long tunnels, and when we got to Genoa, we embarked on the SS *Caserta* and went on to Naples. There the boat filled up. We were down below, in third class, in a long dormitory. The cots were stacked about four high, one on top of the other. Most of the time, the portholes were under water.

We had two guns on the ship. This was wartime in Europe, and there were submarines in the waters. When we were quite a distance from Genoa, everyone was ordered below. They tried out the guns. The vibration was terrific when the guns went off; it shook the whole ship. When we got in the middle of the ocean, one of the sailors who manned the guns thought he saw a submarine and panicked, but it was only the top of a whale. It took us sixteen days to cross the Atlantic. We zigzagged to avoid any enemy ships, and before we got to the Strait of Gibraltar, everyone was warned not to make any noise and not to show any lights. After we left Gibraltar, we were in safe waters.

When I first saw the Statue of Liberty, it was in the evening. The most amazing sight to me was the tall buildings, with their windows lit, just like a fantasyland. Before we got off the boat we were all examined. Then they put us on a ferry. All of us had name tags on our coats. When we got to Ellis Island, my sisters and I were separated from my family. It was pretty sad and scary, and my mother didn't know for a couple of days where the kids went. They took me to the hospital because I had a slight cold, red eyes, and low-grade fever. The second day I was there I noticed this old man. He took two tongue depressors and made a cross out of them. He got at the end of the bed, and he would kneel with this for a long time, every day, just kneel and pray. The poor man was so scared and lost. No one to talk to.

They fed us every day, three times a day. Each time we were fed they took head counts. They treated us fine, except we got oatmeal for breakfast, with brown sugar. I didn't know what it was, so I couldn't get myself to eat it. I put it on the windowsill and let the birds eat it.

My sisters and I, we all got better at pretty much the same time, and then we were brought back to our mother. Then we boarded the train to Chicago, and before we took off, they gave my mother a lunch bag consisting of salami, bread, bananas, and a few oranges, enough for the trip to Chicago. And boy did we enjoy it. I'd never seen a banana before!

My father was waiting for us at the train station in Chicago. I hadn't seen him for a couple of years. He took us to my uncle and aunt. We lived with them until we got settled. In the meantime, my mother and dad and my older sister were able to find work. I was left at home. I had to do all the chores: the cooking and the baking and the washing and the babysitting.

When I first went to school, I couldn't understand English, and during recess time I would sit outside, with my old country clothes on. The kids would poke fun at you, and call you "Wop" and "Dago." Eventually the kids started calling me "Rusty." It made me feel like I belonged. They put me into kindergarten. The teacher found out that I was good with clay, making figurines. So she asked me to make animals and put them on the windowsill, and I eventually learned a few words.

The last school I went to was run by nuns. Mother Cabrini had founded it. I knew how to speak a few words in English by then, but it was broken English. So they would give me elocution lessons once a week, which helped a lot. I went to school for two years, and then my dad got a permit for me to work. I was fifteen years old, and I've kept working ever since.

We did any work we could find. We all lived at home, among the Italians. Eventually my father was able to buy a house near the North Side of Chicago. I stayed there for a few years until I got married.

My wife and I got an apartment for a couple of years, and then my brother-in-law and I bought a house for a down payment of fifteen hundred dollars. We had three apartments. We rented one. My cousin had a candy store on the North Side. I learned to make candy and ice cream. The hours were long, fourteen, fifteen hours a day. After thirteen years I couldn't hack it anymore. I got a job downtown at the Maurice L. Rothschild Department Store.

I waited quite a long time to become a citizen (in 1936), but I was happy when I did it. I felt like I was somebody. I felt like an American, even before I got my citizenship papers. It meant an awful lot to me to be able to be in this country. Whatever I have achieved here wouldn't have been possible in Europe.

MARION DA RONCA spent his first nine years in Vigo, in the Venetian Alps, near the Austrian border. His father, a heavy drinker, had left the family when the boy was quite small, and his mother and two sisters made do as best as they could in rented quarters. German troops occupied his town toward the end of World War I. His oldest sister had immigrated to the United States before the war started and invited her mother and her younger siblings to join her and her husband on their farm in Wisconsin. They sailed in 1920.[4]

The only thing we packed was our clothes. That's all there was to pack. We traveled ten to fifteen miles on a horse-drawn carriage, then boarded a train to Padua and Terrine in Italy. Then we boarded a train to Cherbourg, France. The following evening the tide came in and they ferried us out to the boat. We traveled third class. We were on the back end. They all got sick except me. I watched the dolphins following the ship. You could hear them jumping off out of sight.

As we entered the harbor in New York, I saw the Statue of Liberty. We stood on the side of the ship and my mother told me, "Remember her. For years to come, you will be thinking about her." And she was right. Everyone stood up and took their caps off when they went by. And the tugboats were waiting for us. They pulled alongside, and they pushed the boat right into port. Then they ferried us to Ellis Island.

We were all examined, and then we stayed overnight. We had four bunk beds. There was one for my mother, one for me, then one for each of my sisters, all in one room. And they were hard, covered with just a couple of blankets. We ate in the big dining room. My mother had me by the hand all the while. She never let go as long as we were there.

When we left Ellis Island, we went back to the ferry and then took a train out from New York Central to Detroit. We changed trains in Detroit and went to Chicago. In Chicago, they bussed us around the lake to the Northwestern Station and from there we went to Hurley, Wisconsin. We stayed over at my sister's. I went to school the following fall, and in about five to six months I was talking pretty good English. I learned the cursing words first. They were the ones the kids teach you first.

The people in our community came from many nationalities. There were Belgians, Poles, Swedes, Finns, and Italians. Most ended up in the mines of northern Minnesota, the Upper Peninsula of Michigan, and northern Wisconsin. Most of the children when they started first grade did not know a word of English. They spoke their parents' language at home.

I was eighteen years old when I went logging in the woods. I was twenty-three when I started working in the mines. Copper mining was easy; there was a lot of machinery. Iron mining was bad. I spent forty years in iron mines underground. The first bad job I had in the mines was drilling and blasting, making tunnels into the ore body. When the mine closed down we were down forty-two hundred feet.

My wife was born in the Iron Belt. We went to school together, same grade. We are both happy here. Sometimes my heart longs for Italy. I was back there some twenty years ago, and it was nice to go over there, but here is my home, here. My family is here. Over there, I would not want to go back to live there—no, no, no, no. I stay here. This is my home.

ANNETTE TERLIZZI MONOUYDAS was born in a small town at the outskirts of Naples. In 1928 she immigrated with her mother and two brothers to the United States. She was eight years old when she saw her father for the first time. He had left Italy after the end of World War I and became an engineer on a railroad between New York and Chicago. After he contracted TB, he settled in upstate New York and opened up a hot dog stand. Then he sent for his family.[5]

My mother did most of the packing, whatever we took, which wasn't much. We had no toys. When we got to the ship, I was ready to get on, but they found one little bug in my hair, and they wouldn't let me go through. So we had to go all the way back home. We got rid of the bug, and then we started all over again. We boarded the *Conte Biancamano*. To me, the ship looked huge, and so did the waves.

It took us nine days to get to New York. The ship was swaying back and forth, and on the third day, everybody was real sick. We were on the lowest deck, the cheapest. Our family was in one big room with bunk beds. You just stayed there in that room, and if you went out, you just walked around—one hallway here and one hallway there. We came to New York around noon, and everybody was yelling, "There's the Statue of Liberty, the Statue of Liberty, the Statue of Liberty!"

We had to wait for our trunks. They had to unload them off the ship. And then we were taken to one big room, and there were so many people, screaming and yelling and hugging. My mother was looking to find my father, who was a perfect stranger to me. He hugged and kissed me. I kind of hugged back a little. In a way I was sort of scared. We stayed overnight with relatives in New York City. They cooked dinner for us that evening.

The next morning we had to leave to go to Loon Lake. That's where we were going to make our home. It was very, very lonesome up there. The closest town was twelve miles away. It had ten homes. Saranac Lake was seventeen miles away, Plattsburg was thirty-five miles, and Malone was thirty-six miles away. To us it was like the end of the world. We had to walk a mile to school. It was a one-room schoolhouse. One teacher taught everybody. At first the kids were making fun of us when they couldn't understand us. After a while they got used to us, and they started playing games with us.

My father spoke broken English, and my brothers and I tried to teach my mother. Everything we learned in school we tried to teach her, because she was going to be with the public all the time. My mother's job was selling hot dogs, pumping gas, or putting oil in the car because my father had started a service station, selling cigarettes, hot dogs, ice cream, and candy. That's how he started off, real small.

My father was always in business of some kind. During Prohibition time, my two older brothers and I had to hide bootlegged whiskey in the woods. We dug holes and covered it up in different spots, and then when people came, it was up to us to go and dig it out, whether it was raining or storming or snowing. And that's how my mother got caught. She was sitting in a chair, a blanket over her lap hiding the whiskey bottles underneath, but someone must have squealed on her. The state troopers came on big horses, stopped at our business, pulled up her blanket, and they had the evidence right there. They took her to jail in Malone. She was gone for three days. She thought she was never going to get out of there; she was afraid she would be there for the rest of her life.

When we first came here, we didn't even have a home. We had to stay in a tent. That's where my two brothers and I slept. My father had just a hot dog stand and one little room back there for him and my mother. Then he rented a house about three miles down the road, and we walked back and forth for three winters. Then he finally started building a home. And of course we still had the grocery stand and the service station. When the Prohibition days were over, he got a license to sell beer and liquor. Then he started building a dance hall, which turned into a night club. The people who stayed at the Loon Lake Hotel used to come to our place to drink and dance and eat.

We worked hard here in this country, my two brothers and I. When we were only kids we had to cut down our own wood, cut our own ice and put it in the ice house, and we used to watch the young people come to our business to have fun. Everybody was having fun. But us, all we had to do, it seems, was just work, go to school and work, go to school and work. That's all we used to do. And the business was seven days a week, so you are just with the public, day in and day out. I think of myself as an American now, I've been here so many years.

RITA COSTA FINCO was thirteen years old when she emigrated with her mother in 1929. She was born in northern Italy in Asiago, a town that the Germans had bombed during World War I. She remembered the sleigh rides she took during the winter and an encounter with Benito Mussolini when he came to town.[6]

I was about ten years old, and Mussolini came to town to dedicate a monument. And we had to write an essay about him. My parents were not happy with Mussolini. My dad hated him with a passion. I wrote essay in school, and I got the bronze medal. So at the dedication, I was supposed to go there. My mother refused to send me, and my aunt said, "No way." So I didn't go to school that day.

My dad had to disappear a lot, and we couldn't figure out where he was going, because everything was hush-hush. Later on, when we came to the United States, I found out that he used to hide in the mountains when the special police came to town. My dad went to America, and after five years he became a citizen. For five years, my mother got a check from him every month. He waited until he got his papers, and they couldn't deny us the passport.

We went by train to Genoa, and then we boarded the ship *Roma*. We all got sick. It was eleven days of rough waters. Going through Ellis Island was a nightmare. The doctors checked you over, and Mother got quite upset because I had a scar on my arm from a vaccination and they suspected that I was carrying something. They finally let us through. When we disembarked, there was an Italian American benefit society that took care of people getting off the boat, and they took us to a boardinghouse where we stayed overnight. In the morning they came and took us to the train. They were very nice people.

We got off in Chicago, and then we went on to Ironwood, Michigan. My mother and I were the only ones going up to the Upper Peninsula. We had a big party, and my dad had a house waiting for us to move in. At that time, he worked in the iron mine. It closed down during the Depression. And life became very hard.

It took me some two years to learn the English language. I went to a Catholic school, and the sisters took a lot of time with me: "See Jane Run. See Spot." They were surprised that I could do math, but numbers are the same in Italian and English. Then came the Depression, and you had to do without new shoes and without a new dress. I remember going to the high school prom, and one of my relatives knitted a dress for me.

When I graduated from high school I worked in the office and in the afternoon in the kitchen of an old age home near Ironwood. Then my fiancé got a job in Cleveland, and we got married and raised our first two children there. Then we moved to Cudahy, Wisconsin, to work in a plant that makes engines for airplanes.

Now I have four kids and nine grandchildren. We lead a simple life. I got so emotional when we went to Ellis Island,

and I saw my name on the Wall of Honor. I am happy that I am here in this country.

SUNDAY (DOMENICA) CALABRESA WOOD was eleven years old when she came to America with her mother and a younger brother in 1932. Her father had already been in the United States for ten years, working in construction. She was born in southern Italy, in Calabria, and was in the fourth grade when she left.[7]

I went to a one-room schoolhouse. In front of the room there was the desk of the professor. And there were the pictures—the picture of Moses and of Mussolini—and there was a cross. And there was a blackboard catty-corner. And whenever somebody didn't behave, the teacher would put them behind the blackboard. We had one very tall fellow, and every time he didn't behave he was put behind the blackboard, and we'd see his feet and his head, and we used to go hysterical laughing.

In my village I saw a lot of poverty, but we were comfortable because Papa was sending us money from America and my great-grandmother owned land. We prepared for about a year before we left. My mother prepared beautiful embroidered bedding and a few beautiful spreads. She brought a ceramic clock and a coffee pot with little cups. We had two suitcases and a steamer trunk. I left my doll and my clothes to a girlfriend who was very poor. My mother made new clothes for us to come to America.

The whole town accompanied us when we left. After a half mile they started bidding us good-bye, and my grandmother and great-grandmother cried. It was a sad farewell. We walked up and down the hills till we reached the city of Mileto, where we boarded the train. My grandfather bought our railroad tickets to Naples, and I still have a vivid memory of him with his big white handkerchief and the tears rolling down from his eyes.

We stayed in Naples for three days, waiting for a document that finally came through the Teletype. We boarded the ship *Roma* at the last minute. Our quarters were very comfortable: four bunk beds in each little room and a sink. For meals we went into a huge dining room that the adults used for dancing in the evening. On the far side there was a piano. There was a lot of comfortable seating. And that's where we spent most of our days, listening to the piano and conversing. And there was another room adjoining it. In there we went for church services in the morning, and in the afternoon they showed Charlie Chaplin movies. We played hopscotch on the deck. On good sunny days we saw whales rising in the ocean.

As we approached New York Harbor, we first saw the Statue of Liberty. Everyone up on deck started to holler, "La libertà, la libertà! Viva la libertà!" I thought it was a saint protecting the port, and in my mind's eye I thought we were going to live in one of the tall buildings. At Ellis Island we met my father, and after the hugging and kissing, this nun walks past and sticks a little religious book in my hand. As she put it in my hands, she said, "Gratis, gratis." I knew in Latin that meant "free, free."

Then we entered a large room with a wooden staircase, and we were at the counter where the doctor examined our eyes and throats. I remember we walked a little and then we got on a little boat. We docked at Ellis Island in the morning when the sun was shining. When we arrived in Freeport by taxi, the sun was still shining.

I started school in September. I was put in the first grade because I did not speak the language. The principal came into the classroom one day and brought a sign that said, "Silence." I raised my hand when she asked us to read, and I said, "Silenzi!" The kids were very friendly. Later I had more relatives come in and they were put in my class because I could translate for them. I skipped grades. As soon as I learned the language I was put in the third grade. Then the following year I did the fourth and fifth grades and then the sixth grade. I started the seventh grade, but I left during the Depression time. I went to work in the Garment District. I took the train in Freeport and enjoyed it very much, going to Manhattan. I worked there for eight years, and then I met my husband and married him. Eventually we had a beautiful home in Freeport. While I was working in the city I walked over to the Metropolitan Opera House on Broadway, and I took singing lessons. Also, I was always interested in writing. During the past five years I wrote a novel called *40 Million Ducats*. It has to do with life in the old country and the experience of coming to America. I had several stories published in small presses and newspapers, and I intend to continue. Right now, at age seventy-one, I am in the process of doing a lot of writing. This is my life right now, writing.

SANDY (SANTA) LORETTA LOCOCO MAZZA came from Sicily in 1937. She was six years old at the time and had attended convent school in the fishing village of Porticello. Her father had already immigrated to the United States and worked for a coal company, loading coal on trucks. He lived with his sister and her nine children in Milwaukee, and sent for his wife and child when he had saved enough money for their passage.[8]

> We got on a carriage, and we drove to Palermo, and then we boarded the ship. It was a luxury liner, so it offered good food and good accommodations. When the ship came into New York Harbor, and we saw the Statue of Liberty, my mother said, "At last I am free!" My uncle met us at Ellis Island, and we boarded a train to Buffalo. I remember our first Christmas—I got a little stove, which was darling—and seeing snowflakes come down, and we spent New Year's Eve with my uncle who had picked us up in New York. We stayed with my aunt once we came to Wisconsin, for a couple of weeks, and then my father managed to get a house across the street from them.
>
> My difficulties at the time were the language barrier. I knew no English, and there was no one to really help me out. I was placed in a school where the nuns came from Italy. I was the only immigrant child in my class. There was a nun at St. Rita's who really took a liking to me, but unfortunately she was transferred. All of a sudden I withdrew, because the children would laugh at the way I spoke and how I pronounced words when I read.
>
> I became the caregiver in my family because I was the translator. I went to all the doctors' appointments. I went to the market with my mother. I was taking her place instead of her taking mine. My mother and dad tried to go to night school, but not too long. My mother tried more than my father. He was too busy making money and supporting the family, just making a living. My mother was a very progressive woman. She took to America like you would not believe. Both of my parents had a

love of America and were very, very grateful to be here.

I graduated from high school and went on to trade school. I was married to an Italian and had a baby. After my last child was old enough to go to school and take care of himself, I went back to being a hairdresser. I would have loved to have been an elementary schoolteacher. But I really feel America is my homeland and I get very emotional about it.

My husband, Nick, has given me all the confidence in the world. He is my best friend. I am happy about the accomplishments of my children. One is a dentist, one is a very accomplished advertising executive, Nick is in merchandising, and my daughter, Pam, is wonderful. What I love about America is that everybody is on one level. Everybody can be friends with everybody else. I love Italy, but I wouldn't want to live there. They haven't got tolerance for a lot of things you find here. I am very lucky person to live here.

5

St. Olaf's Children from Scandinavia

Some 1.3 million immigrants from Scandinavia passed through Ellis Island between 1892 and 1954. Among them were Swedish, Danish, Norwegian, and Finnish children and teenagers who joined family members who had come before them. Some arrived as orphans, but all hoped to find a better life in the land across the sea. Low wages and crop failures pushed many young people out of their homeland. The emigration was so massive that it left some towns and villages in Sweden half empty.[1]

Most sailed in third-class cabins on the ships of the Scandinavian-American Line from Copenhagen, Göteborg, and Oslo to New York. Some would stay in the eastern United States, especially New England. Many more would head for the Great Plains in the Midwest and settle in Illinois, Wisconsin, Minnesota, North and South Dakota, Nebraska, Kansas, and Iowa. Others would venture to Montana and the faraway state of Washington.

As young adults, thousands of Scandinavian immigrants who had passed through Ellis Island as boys fought in the armed forces. And there were young women as well—like Thyra Pearson, who had immigrated in 1916 at age seven—who volunteered to serve in World War II. She joined the Women's Army Auxiliary

Corps (WAAC) and rose to the rank of master sergeant.[2]

I was born in Kristianstad, Sweden. My father came to the United States five years before my mother, my brother, my sister, and I did. We lived in an old brick building that looks a lot like the farmhouses they have nowadays in Sweden, a great big red barn. My mother and we children lived at one end of the building; my grandparents lived at the other end. My mother worked at the local school, cleaning; my grandmother helped take care of us. My grandfather worked for a farmer with a big estate, just across the road from us. My father ended up working on a farm in North Dakota after trying his luck in Montana and Minnesota. He finally sent money for my mother to come on a boat.

We had to have physical examinations prior to going on board ship in Göteborg. We came third class. My brother and I had to sleep in the upper bunks, and my mother and sister down at the bottom. My mother made some very good friends on the trip, but we were separated in Ellis Island when we arrived after nine or ten days. When we got to Ellis Island we were ushered into a large room that reminded me of a railroad station because there were a lot of benches for people to sit and wait for their papers to be cleared so they could continue on their trip. We were detained for four days.

One thing that was comfortable was our sleeping quarters. We would line up and be issued a blanket and a pillow for each of us. They were real hot at the time. We learned that they were put in ovens during the day so that they could kill any lice or vermin people might have. Each family was assigned to a little sleeping compartment. And in the dining room you were assigned to a table. There would be a chunk of bread and some fruit by each place, but some of the women had little bags and would just grab somebody else's apple and bread, put them into their bag, and take them to their own table. We sat around and played with the other children who waited. We got to play with a little ball, and my mother had a couple of toys for us. We played and killed time and waited. After four days my mother was called in and the inspectors said, "You have been cleared and here is your ticket, and you can continue on your trip." So we took the train to Minneapolis, and that's where my father met us. We spent about two weeks with my father's brother and wife and their two small children before we went to North Dakota.

When we came up there, we had to live with the farmer that my father was working for. My mother helped the lady of the house as best she could with cooking and cleaning during the summer months. During the fall my dad got a small farm about half a mile away. And that's where we lived in a small house for several years.

We raised all kinds of grain—wheat, rye, oats, and barley—and we always raised lots of potatoes. We had our own garden and did our own canning. And it was my brother's and my job to milk the cows in the morning and evenings and to churn the milk before we could take off for school. We had a two-mile walk to school.

There was one Swedish family that lived not too far away from us, and their two children, a boy and a girl, spoke a little Swedish and helped us a little bit when we went to school. But it didn't take me very long to pick up the language. My dad could speak a little bit of English by that time, and my mother was very interested in learning the language, so when we came home with our books to study, she took the little time she had to study with us. I lived in North Dakota for eight years. I finished grammar school there, and then I came to Chicago to live with my aunt, a relative of my mother's.

My aunt had told me that when I finished grammar school I could come to her and she would send me to business school. And so I did. I took a stenographic course and then I answered an ad in the *Tribune*. I first worked in a real estate office and got a very nice recommendation from them. Then I worked for Butler Brothers, a wholesale company, for a number of years and then for a pharmaceutical company in Evanston, Illinois.

One Saturday when I got off work, I read about the Women's Army Auxiliary Corps. I took a ride downtown, and they signed me up and told me to come in for a physical exam the next Wednesday. And when I came to work on Monday, I told them, "I won't be in on Wednesday because I have an examination. I am planning on joining the army." They gave me a beautiful watch when I left, and two weeks later I was sworn into the armed services. I took a train down to Georgia and went for basic training. After that they sent me to an administration school in Conway, Arkansas, for six weeks, and then I was assigned to a job at Sheppard Field, Texas. I spent three years there.

I went up in rank pretty fast. When the war ended, I reenlisted and worked for several years at the Fitzsimmons General Hospital in Denver, Colorado, near where my sister lived. Finally in 1953, came a request for a master sergeant in Europe. So I went to Germany and spent two years there. And during that time I made two trips to Sweden. I have a lot of cousins over there. It seems to me they live a lot better than any of my brothers and sisters or any of my relatives over here. They all have beautiful homes and gardens, and most have a summer home, besides.

But as much as I loved it over there and would love to make another trip back there, I feel like my mother did: this is my country, and here is where I want to be.

EDWARD RUNE MYRBECK came with his adoptive family in 1923 from Sweden to the United States. He was twelve years old. After a lifetime of accomplishments and service, this son of an immigrant bricklayer was knighted by the king of Sweden.[3]

Shortly after my birth, my mother became very sick. She died when I was about a year and a half old, and the Myrbeck family adopted me. I grew up in a poor agricultural area in the south, in a place where when God created Sweden he threw all the rocks there. During World War I, we did not have much food, and we ate a lot of turnips. I remember my parents picking dandelion roots, baking them in the oven, and cutting them up and mixing them with coffee. And then after the war, there was the Depression, and that's one of the reasons why my dad decided to leave the country. He had relatives in Boston, and all my mother's relations were in Rockford, Illinois.

I was very excited about going to America. I thought I was going to see Indians. I had read Mark Twain, and I was excited about seeing a Negro. We sold everything we owned at a daylong auction—all the furniture, all the toys, all the trivia. We had nothing left except our clothes. Before you left you had to have a passport photo. My aunt Anna had sent me a nice suit with knickers from America, and I didn't have a shirt that was good enough to put underneath that suit. So my grandmother brought out a beautiful white linen towel and wrapped it around my neck and put my suit coat on.

My father left first and got a job as a bricklayer. He sent for us about six months later. My mother traveled alone with three children: a one-and-a-half-year-old on her arm, a five-year-old who held onto her hand, and a twelve-year-old who didn't know how to behave. We had a couple of trunks with personal effects but not much.

We took the boat in Copenhagen. We got there by train from the west coast of Sweden. We went third class; the food was excellent. It was the first time in my life that I had oranges. I got to know some other children who traveled second class, and they filled my pockets with fruit—oranges and bananas. It was a nice boat with running water and central heating and switches on the wall that made the lights go on. I think that's what got me interested in electronics, which became my profession afterward for all my life.

I remember seeing the Statue of Liberty when we pulled into New York Harbor. "Frihetsgudinnan," they called it, or "Freedom Goddess." What got me more excited than anything else was to see the electric lights, especially in the evening, and a melee of people and languages. It's an odd situation for a young kid to come into a place where you have absolutely no knowledge of what people are saying. Somebody would look at you and say something, and you'd just shake your head.

I was not at all frightened; I was just enthralled by the whole thing. We got into the harbor on the boat in the evening, and there were these flashing lights that would come on and off, off and on, in different colors. I remember one sign especially—LIPTON— and then t-e-a, and then c-o-c-o-a, and then c-o-f-f-e-e: Lipton's Tea, Cocoa, and Coffee. Now there was my first English lesson.

And then we took the train from Grand Central Station to the Midwest—to Chicago and on to Rockford. The reason for going to Rockford, where we met my uncles, was that it used to be a community primarily of Swedes. It was nice because I could understand what everybody was talking about. I remember walking and talking with my uncle Axel, and I asked him what a gum machine was. He said, "That's candy."

It was the first time I ever had chewing gum, and I chewed and chewed and chewed and tried to talk at the same time. I walked at least a mile and a half, and I kept chewing all the time. Finally I thought, I'd better swallow this. This doesn't look good for me, chewing.

Christmas comes along. You go to the stores. You look in. The old Tinker Toys, things you would love to have. Electric trains, steam engines—oh, if you could have only one of those. But it did not occur to you that was for you. That was inbred for you. What you got for Christmas was clothes—stockings, a shirt. I got my first bicycle when I was about fourteen or fifteen.

I started school about a week or two after I got to Rockford. They put me in kindergarten on a chair about twelve inches high. They finally got me a regular chair. There are things on the blackboard that you don't understand, but finally after a week they decide that you must be bright enough to get into the second class. And then you go into the third class, and you consider yourself real smart. Everybody makes fun of you when you get out into the schoolyard. They called me "Swede" and "Square Head." But it didn't take me long to learn the English language reasonably well. I think I learned English in about six or seven months.

You ask me today, when I am seventy-five years old, whether I am Swedish or an American. I am an American. After sixty-three years in this country I can't be anything but an American. I have been back to Sweden five times. When I see the American flag there I say, "That's where I belong!" When I see the Swedish flag here, I have a certain warm feeling for it. If I didn't have that feeling I wouldn't have been as involved as I have been in the Swedish community in the United States. And I wouldn't have been knighted by the king of Sweden.

I have been on the board of directors of my electronics company for over thirty-five years. I have been head of the Independent Order of Vikings and their national president. I am in the American Masonic Lodge and in the Swedish Masonic Lodge. I started a club for Swedish Americans, and it is the biggest club in membership in the whole United States except for

the Irish. We have done something for the American people: we
have contributed to the melting pot.

I speak well of Sweden. I speak with the feeling that it is a
good country. But nobody can say to me, "Why don't you go
back there?" Because I don't belong there. I belong here.

MARTHA HOGLIND, daughter of a Danish mother and a Swedish
father, came to the United States at age seven on board the SS *Hellig
Olav* in 1927. That ship, built for the Scandinavian-American Line,
sailed regularly from its home port of Copenhagen to Oslo and then
to New York and back again. When they sailed, Martha, her mother,
and her two brothers were among the ship's nine hundred third-
class passengers. Her father had left in 1926 to find a job as an elec-
trician in the United States and saved enough money so that his
family could come over a year later.[4]

I grew up in a red brick house in the southern part of Jutland, a
great big house that belonged to my (maternal) grandfather. He
was a delight. He always dressed in black, wore a black hat,
and smoked a long pipe. He walked up and down the streets of
his little town in his big wooden shoes, followed by his little
dog.

I went to school for one term in my own little wooden shoes.
I took them off before we went into the classroom, and we wrote
on slates. At recess, in the middle of the morning we would go
home and get a piece of pumpernickel with sugar on it. In the
winter we went ice-skating on a pond outside our town. At
Christmastime we would have a goose and red cabbage, brown
potatoes with sugar, and sweet candied white potatoes, and an
ice cream cone and orange. On December 23, "Little Christmas
Eve," we put our shoes outside the door, and they put oranges
in there.

When we left, my little brother Hanz looked up at my
grandfather and said, "You mustn't cry, Grandpa. I'll be back
in twenty years." And I said good-bye to our baker; that's the
only person I remember saying good-bye to. We took our feather
beds with us. They kept us warm in our cabin. We did have a
porthole, and I remember how the seats on our cushions were
sliding during a storm. We were all seasick, but they announced

that they were going to give us ice cream and oranges to eat, so of course we recovered.

When we arrived in New York, we went to Jersey City. We stayed with my aunt and uncle who was my mother's brother. I had to wait about six months before I entered school, but I skipped some grades and went to summer school so I could get up to the right class for my age group. I can't remember that it was difficult for me to learn English.

My mother and father worked as janitors for a while. My mother was the ambitious one; she wanted to go and see the world. So they opened up a boardinghouse in Brooklyn. We rented out eight rooms. My mother died there at age thirty-eight, when I was twelve years old. Then I had to keep house after school, clean the house, and wash the dishes. I hated it. I couldn't keep it up. Eventually we moved to a nice apartment building but then came the Depression. And we moved to the tenements, the railroad flats.

This was not the nicest part of my life. In the front part of our living room and in the back, there was a brick wall of about two feet, and the kitchen had a wooden stove and an icebox. And the water was always running all over the floor. But we had a kind Italian iceman who would bring us wine for Christmas, with the ice, and Mrs. Hansen, a friend of the family, came once a week to teach me how to cook.

I resented it deeply that I could not join the other children in play, but starting at sixteen, I had fun folk dancing. We danced in Hartford, and we danced in Bridgeport, and we danced in the big restaurants in New York with our folk dance group. We didn't go out during the week, because we had three hours' homework to do every night. We went out Friday or Saturday night. The Danes and the Swedes would all get together, and once in a while we'd go to the Italian club, with those beautiful dark-haired Italians. We danced with the Poles and in the Finn Hall with all the sailors from the different Scandinavian countries. Each ethnic group had their own clubs.

I finished grammar school and graduated from high school. I should have gone on to college. Most of the time I kept house, but then I worked in department stores and for the World's Fair in 1938. When the war broke out, both of my brothers went in the service. Hanz was a Marine; Knute worked on an experimental ship when they tested the A-bomb off the Bikini Islands. I went and worked for the Department of Defense. After the war I worked for the Swedish consulate as a switchboard operator.

Then, one day, I saw in the paper an ad: "Secretary wanted overseas." I took the Civil Service test and worked for the government in Japan, Denmark, France, and Germany for about twelve years altogether and then in the States for about ten years. I am very patriotic. I became less prejudiced by working for the American government overseas. I always wanted something different from the ordinary. Well, I got that. I had a pretty good life!

ASTA M. ANDERSEN HOGLIND, at seven years of age, came from Denmark with her mother and two brothers on the SS *Frederik VIII*, and eventually met and married Martha's older brother Knute.[5]

I was born in Copenhagen. We lived on the fourth floor of an apartment building, my mother, my two brothers, and myself. My (maternal) grandparents lived in the countryside in a house with a thatched roof. My grandfather was a shoemaker, and he had his little shop in the back of the house. My grandmother had a vegetable garden, filled with vines and fruits that she canned. The minute school closed in Copenhagen, we headed there. We traveled from Copenhagen by train to Roskilde and then by bus.

My parents were estranged because my father was an alcoholic. He had a very good position as a mailman, and he lost his job because he left his bag of letters in a hallway outside his area. So he went to the United States. He came back for a couple of weeks and talked my mother into going back with him to this country, but he did not send us any money. My mother supported us by sewing on her machine.

I started school in Denmark. I went for about half a year before we came to the United States. I am left-handed, and they did not permit that in the Danish school system at the time. My brother used to have to sit with me and force me to write right-handed. As the boys were getting older, my mother thought they would not be getting any higher education in Denmark.

Sure, we knew people had children who went to college, but we were not in that socio-economic class. She felt the boys would have more opportunities in the States.

My mother bought four tickets, and my brother Paul, the younger of the two boys, took them to school to prove we were leaving. My mother was hysterical. She couldn't find the tickets until he brought them back. We packed two big crates with bedding and clothes. We also had suitcases that we brought on board ship and her sewing machine.

We came across on the SS *Frederik VIII*, a ship that was top heavy and rolled a lot.

We were all in one cabin in third class. The Poles were the ones who ended up in steerage. They came on board in Copenhagen, carrying their clothing, their bedding, and their sheets on their backs. They were very poor and were put in the lowest part of the ship. We sailed toward the end of March and were plenty seasick.

On April 1, our ship anchored at Hoboken, New Jersey. We went on a small boat to Ellis Island. For the physical exam, the boys had to go separately, and my mother was upset. She didn't know if we would ever meet again. She and I had to go to the women's section, and we were stripped, and they examined us, especially our eyes. They took a pencil and wrapped our eyelids around it to check for disease, but we had no such problems. Denmark was a pretty progressive country even then, and we always had access to a doctor.

After the examination, our father met us in the Registry Room behind a big desk. We went on a small boat to Battery Park and passed the Statue of Liberty. My father had rented an apartment in Brooklyn. In the back was a feed store, and we had plenty of mice that climbed up the curtains. It was awful, but we didn't live there very long. My uncle, a brother of my father's, found us a better apartment on East Third Street among people whose parents had been Danish immigrants.

There was a school about a block away, P.S. 10, and my uncle got us enrolled there. I would go out to play and the kids would surround me, and they were asking, "Ocha nien?" They were saying, "What's you name?" Learning to read in English was a little hard, but there were some Scandinavians who helped me, especially Uncle Tony. He fixed up a nice carriage for my first Christmas, and then he would sit with me because I wasn't progressing very fast to help me overcome the language barrier. So after all that, I went through grade school and to the Girls' Commercial High School. And since coming to Florida, I have college credits as well, so I did get an education.

My first job was during the Depression. I was a switchboard operator, and then I became a bookkeeper. I got into a Danish folk dance group, and that's where I met my husband. There were two Danish churches in Brooklyn, and they weren't very far apart, maybe eight or ten blocks. Martha and her brother went to one; I went to the other. Their church had dancing, and that's where I met Knute and Martha, of course.

It was a large group, and we had a home on Long Island we rented and where we could go in the summertime. There was boating and swimming. The girls all stayed in the big house, and the boys went to the barn, where they had their cots all lined up.

We had a lot of good times in those two Danish churches. We had Christmas tree parties where the big tree was put up, and we danced around it in the traditional style. I went to Sunday school and was confirmed in Salem Church. I made friends there with another Danish girl, Lillian, who had come over as a twelve-year-old immigrant.

It was the nicest time in our lives, really. I married Knute in that church. That was our life—the church. Not that we were religious fanatics, but it was a place to meet nice people, contemporaries. Now I have one daughter, Judith, and a grandson, John Christopher. We call him "J. C." We live well enough here. After all I am a Dane.

INGRID AHLFORS came to the United States from Finland in 1914, at age twelve, in the company of an aunt. Her father had died when she was four years old, and her mother had left with an older sister to try her luck in America when Ingrid was seven years old.[6]

> We were poor. Father worked in a sawmill. After my father died, my mother went to work in a cotton mill. About three years later she decided to immigrate to America with my sister to join

my father's brother and his family. She left my brother and me in the care of my grandmother because she didn't think she could take three children at once.

I went to a one-room school for a while. There was no electricity; we studied by kerosene lamps. People got around on horseback through muddy streets. I left with my aunt who had come to visit on a cold December day. I remember the walk to the railroad station through the snow and the cold. I just carried a few clothes. We took the train to Rauma.

From Rauma we took a small freighter. There were no accommodations for passengers. People were lying down in the hold. We were supposed to take off the night when we got to Rauma, but there was a blizzard, so the captain said we would have to wait. We took off the next morning, and it was a very stormy passage to Stockholm. We got to Sweden some time after dark. We were taken to a hotel to sleep overnight. From Stockholm we took the train to Malmö at the southern tip of Sweden. Then we took a ferry across to Copenhagen, and there we got on board the liner *United States*.

When we first went on board, the captain invited us to go into his little cabin to sit down, but we weren't there very long before I got seasick. I was flat on my back the whole trip.

We were in steerage. We had a cabin with several bunk beds. It accommodated four people: my aunt and I and a woman with a little boy who were traveling at the same time as us. We sailed on December 10, and we came into Ellis Island on December 25—Christmas Day.

In the big building, my aunt and I and the woman with the little boy were put into a separate wire-enclosed area. During the afternoon we children were taken into an inside play area, with swings and seesaws. At mealtime, we were marched over to the dining area, where there were very long tables and benches, and plates that were made of some sort of metal. I was hungry because I hadn't eaten anything throughout the whole voyage. Once I was off the ship, I started to feel better.

We spent two nights at Ellis Island waiting for my mother to come from Fitchburg, Massachusetts, to pick us up. We were taken upstairs to a closed-in room. There were metal springs on posts between the ceiling and the floor, and they were in layers.

There were just the metal springs the first night and we spread out coats and dresses so we wouldn't be too uncomfortable. The second night we had blankets because my aunt complained. There was a Belgian woman in there with us, waiting for her husband to come and claim her and their three children.

After my mother came to claim us, we were taken by boat to New York and from there by subway to Grand Central Station and then by train to Fitchburg. Fitchburg had a regular area where everyone was Finnish. There was plenty of work there and a great need for immigrants because the mills could absorb all the help they could get and you didn't need to speak English to get along.

My mother had an apartment with my sister, and my sister had been going to school. She spoke English fairly well by then. I started school right after January 1. So many immigrants were coming in at that time—some French speaking, a boy from Turkey, a couple of Swedish kids. Whoever came in and couldn't speak English was put in the same room with a teacher who spoke only English. So we had to start learning fast.

Except for the language barrier I felt at home. The winters are pretty severe, but I was used to lots of snow. My mother fairly well stuck to the old food—beef stew, lamb stew, pork chops—but it was more varied. I had never tasted tomatoes or bananas before.

I continued speaking Finnish with my mother because she preferred that. I tried to teach some Finnish to my oldest daughter, but people said, "She'll be confused," so I gave up. My husband is Finnish, too, and we became citizens in the early 1940s. We planned on going to Finland for a visit after he retired, but he was just sixty-one when he died, and then I never went back. I belong here.

6

Survivors of the Armenian Genocide

More than half a million Armenians live in the United States today, concentrated in Greater Boston, New York, Philadelphia, Detroit, Chicago, Fresno, and Los Angeles. Among them are the child survivors of the Armenian genocide who fled their ancient homeland after the massacres that began in 1915 and after subsequent waves of persecution and expulsion between 1920 and 1923. It is estimated that 1.5 million Armenian men, women, and children perished between 1915 and 1923. By 1923, Asia Minor had been expunged of its Armenian population. The destruction of the Christian Armenian communities in this part of the world was total.[1]

The Young Turk government of the Ottoman Empire carried out the Armenians' persecution. It began in April 1915 when hundreds of Armenian professionals and intellectuals were arrested and killed. After these arrests, widespread massacres took place in all parts of Turkey between 1915 and 1918. The great bulk of the Armenian population was forcibly removed to Syria, then under Ottoman rule, and sent on death marches into the desert. After a short period of calm at the end of World War I, the atrocities were renewed between 1920 and 1923, and the remaining Armenians were subjected to further massacres and expulsions. All Armenian property was confiscated.

All the major powers at the time—the United States, Great Britain, France, Russia, and Germany—condemned the Armenian genocide. Diplomats and missionaries stationed in Turkey and Syria wrote anguished accounts of the Armenians' persecution, detailing the sufferings of the children.[2] Among them are reports from Consul J. B. JACKSON, who was stationed in Aleppo during the height of the persecution of the Armenians:

> One of the most terrible sights ever seen in Aleppo was the arrival early in August 1915, of some 5,000 emaciated, dirty, ragged and sick women and children. . . . The number that succumbed in the city was so great that . . . the military authorities provided huge ox carts into which the dead bodies were thrown, 10 or 12 in each cart.

Consul LESLIE DAVIS wrote to Henry Morgenthau, the American ambassador to Turkey in Constantinople: "As one walks through the camps, mothers offer their children and beg one to take them. In fact, the Turks have been taking their choice of these children and girls. . . . They have even had their doctors there to examine and secure the best ones."

ALMA JOHANNSEN, a German missionary, describes how the city of Marash was burned:

> We all had to take refuge in the cellar for fear of our orphanage catching fire. It was heartrending to hear the cries of the people and children who were being burned to death in their houses. . . . I went to the Mutessarif and begged him to have mercy on the children at least, but in vain. He replied that "the Armenian children must perish with their nation."

But some children survived to tell their tales.

VOZCHAN PARSEGIAN (HOVSEPIAN) escaped with his mother and younger sister after enduring the siege of Van and the flight to Yerevan. He managed to reach the United States in 1916 after a long journey by train through Russia and Sweden and then by boat from Liverpool to New York. He was eight years old at the time.[3]

I was born in 1908 in the city of Van in eastern Turkey. My mother and father had been educated in German and American mission schools. They were brought there as orphans. My mother became a cook at the American hospital. My father had been trained as a carpenter and decided to come to the United States after some of his business partnerships didn't work out. Also, they were drafting the Armenian men into the Turkish Army and what happened to them was always a question mark. So he decided to leave after my younger sister was born (in 1912), with the idea of bringing us to the United States eventually.

I went to kindergarten at the same mission school as my parents did. I remember the warmth of the Christmas celebration. It was a joyous occasion for play and music. In the missions it was a happy day. But we were soon aware that the Turkish army had arrived. The city was under siege from April to the end of May 1915. I remember walking through the streets and hearing the bullets and seeing people duck. I remember people scurrying back and forth, and Mother being very busy in the hospital. Somehow the Armenians survived that month.

They survived by organizing everything together with the Germans and Americans. Their real leaders had been killed on April 24, 1915. Now it was the second-level people who helped organize the survival of the group. The city was divided into sections, and individuals were given wet rags and pails and ordered to wait for the cannon balls that were fired by the Turks from the Rock of Van, an old fortress overlooking the city. The Armenians below would watch for these balls to fall, grab the fuses out of the balls, and use the powder for fighting back. About the end of May 1915, the Turkish soldiers left. We went to see what we could salvage. I collected empty shells and one live chicken.

The Turks left because the Russian army was approaching. The Russian general stayed in Van for a while until he and his troops were ordered to the Eastern Front. The general issued orders that everyone must leave. He gave us a day's notice. My sister, my mother, and I started off on a cart, sitting on top of somebody else's furniture. That didn't last long. The rest of the flight had to be on foot. We headed northeast toward Russian Armenia. During the two weeks we were walking, my little

sister was lost. When we arrived in Yerevan, we found the soldier who had the donkey on which she was riding but no
little girl.

    We arrived amid spreading disease and crowding. Dur-
ing the first night there, my mother bought a loaf of bread with
a gold piece she had saved. It was so hard that I couldn't eat it.
Another night she gave a small coin for a shawl to cover me
with. We had hailstones that drew blood. And we had to drink
the water that we walked in and had to pass the water through
whatever rags we had to give it some clearing. But we found
my little sister. Russian soldiers were playing with her.

    Disease was everywhere, cholera and typhoid. The food
carried the disease. My sister and I stopped eating. But one day
we saw a family eating bread dipped in garlic and vinegar, and
we wanted that. We lived on that for two weeks. Meanwhile,
crowds by the thousands came piling in. So my mother went to
the archbishop and offered to cook for the refugees. He gave
her work to cook in an orphanage, and that's where my sister
and I stayed for the next year.

    In time she persuaded the archbishop that she wanted to
leave to get an American education for her children. We got our
passports in a family arrangement that included two additional
couples besides my mother, my sister, and I. Two men had to
pull us children through the window of the train that headed
north from Yerevan. Eventually we arrived in Sweden, and then
somehow we made it to Liverpool, where we took a crowded
ship to America.

    Two weeks before we sailed we got word that my father
had died from an accident. My father's brother met us at Ellis
Island. I remember the crowding there and wondering if we
would be admitted. Fortunately we were in fair health, and my
uncle took us first to New York City and then up to Chelsea,
Massachusetts. My mother immediately got work in a shoe factory. She made six dollars a week; we learned to live on that.

    We always knew how to enjoy Christmas. The house we
lived in had a tree in front. It did have a branch that I could cut
off, and we brought that branch into the house and decorated it
with cotton. That was a real joy I remember, our first Christmas
in the States. My mother was so determined that her children

would get an American education she was willing to take anything, and that's how we survived. I recognized early that this is life. This is what it takes. My mother worked hard, and I was working hard.

Then my mother married a man who had known my father. He was a good man who legally adopted us; therefore, he changed my name to Parsegian. But sadly, he was working on the roof of the house we lived in, fell, broke his back, and died. I was in high school at the time. My mother said, "The first is for you to learn a trade." And so I learned auto repair. One day, while I was repairing a car, a man took the trouble to explain to me that I could study engineering (for free) at the Lowell Institute School, an evening school within the Massachusetts Institute of Technology (MIT) buildings.

After I finished their two-year course I entered the four-year program at MIT. Eventually I went on to a doctorate in nuclear physics and became director of research of the New York office of the Atomic Energy Commission. In the mid-1950s I got an invitation to become the first dean of engineering at the Rensselaer Polytechnic Institute (RPI) in Troy, New York. They wanted somebody who had engineering experience but was in nuclear physics besides. I've been involved with many nuclear issues, and I've appeared many times at hearings with the Joint Committee of Congress on Atomic Energy. And then I got involved with many of the Armenian issues and organized the Armenian Educational Council Incorporated.

The Armenian communities began to be quite concerned about the fact that so little had been said about the massacres and the genocide. So we decided that there should be a public event in Lincoln Center, New York, to commemorate these events. And then, following the examples of the Jews, we began to collect oral histories of those who had lived through the massacres. I have some two hundred tapes that we have passed on to other groups, which are collecting more.

And then came a young architect from Germany who was worried about the Armenian monuments in Turkey and how they could be preserved. And we supported that project with some of the royalties from my books. By then I was about to retire from RPI and the School of Architecture wanted the project to be centered at RPI. I was the only one available to work on this twenty-year project without a salary.

What has stayed with me throughout my life is what my mother taught us: "Just do your best, just do your best." And the moral code and ethics that we grew up with stayed with me.

Thirteen-year-old ALBERT MIAMIDIAN and his six-year-old sister SATINA (PAPAZIAN) came to the United States in 1920 from Syria.[4] They grew up in Aleppo, children of a dry goods merchant. The Turks had persecuted their paternal grandfather and had burned his house in an earlier massacre in 1896, portent of things to come.

ALBERT: When I was in school, the word got out that the Turks were killing thousands of Armenians. The government confiscated my father's stuff, and they killed my grandfather, my uncles, and cousins. They came to our house, looking for my father. He hid behind a sliding door and got out after they left.

SATINA: My husband's parents and his brother and his family were killed during the massacre. He had to bury his father fairly deep, so the dogs wouldn't get the bones.

ALBERT: You go to sleep, and you dream about it. Some people never got over it. I just can't forget all these people dying. I saw it myself with my own eyes. The Turks used to throw all the bodies up in a wagon and carry them all away. I saw all those things with my own eyes. As a kid I was so hungry, I took the grain that they fed the horses in order to survive. So we decided to leave to join an uncle who was in the United States. He was my mother's brother.

SATINA: We brought some Oriental rugs and bedding with us.

ALBERT: We went by train from Aleppo to Beirut, Lebanon, and by boat from Beirut to Marseilles, France.

SATINA: A lot of people got sick on that first boat. But the second boat that went from Marseilles to New York was pretty nice, and we were well treated. Because I was very young they gave me a little snack, something extra.

ALBERT: When we got to Ellis Island, there were lots of gates, lots of questions asked, and they examined us. Then they showed us how to take the train to Philadelphia. My father had enough money with him to take us there. We arrived late at night. My uncle was already asleep when we knocked at his door.

SATINA: He had four children of his own, but he put up with us until we got a little home in Camden, a few blocks away from my uncle's home. There were at least six Armenian families in our block.

ALBERT: They took us around, and they found a job for my father, repairing watches and jewelry. And I went to school and tried to speak English as much as possible. I had to go with my father to the jewelry shop, so I could explain how to get the parts.

SATINA: A teacher used to come and teach my mother English. She taught her how to read and write and how to make flowers. She was a very nice person, very helpful.

ALBERT: I became a citizen and voted for FDR. That was the first time I voted. I served in the army in World War II and was wounded.

SATINA: I became a citizen during the war, after I was married. My husband was a citizen, so I got my citizenship. And my father became a citizen at the same time.

ALBERT: When we passed the Statue of Liberty in the New York Harbor we knew that was it. We are here to stay!

ERVANTHOUHI GARABIDIAN ASSADOURIAN arrived in New York in 1921 at the age of fourteen, accompanied by her cousin Elizabeth.[5] Her grandparents, her mother, her two sisters, and brother had all died in the 1915 massacre of the Armenian community in Kayseri.

I was born in Bunyan, a small village populated mostly by Greeks and Armenians. We were very religious, educated people. My grandfather was the richest man in the village, selling thousands of lambs. We were a large, closely knit family. When the 1915 massacre started, the Turks took my grandparents, my uncles, and all of my family and drove them into the desert.

I was nine years old when the Turks came walking in the garden. Our horse came to me and licked me, with tears in his eyes. I saw some dead bodies near the river. One of them was my mother's mother. I called to her, but there was no answer. I made the sign of the cross, and I prayed for my grandmother.

Some Greek neighbors who knew my grandfather took me to their home and kept me there. My mother's friend, Mrs. Wingate from the American University, put me and some twenty-five other boys and girls in a hiding place. They kept us in a dark place and gave us meals. Later we went to a Turkish orphanage in Kayseri. And then I went to Istanbul and stayed with my uncle, who was an officer in the Turkish army.

I stayed in Istanbul for about three years and went to school there. I had a wonderful time in the years between 1918 and 1920, after World War I ended, but in 1921 the Turks started the killings all over again.

In the meantime, Mrs. Wingate had located my father, who had immigrated to the United States in 1913, and he knew I was alive. My father first sent for my uncle's son, Harry, and then he sent for me. I came on a Turkish ship, the *Gul Djemal*. The trip was pleasant. My cousin, Harry, and my father met me at Ellis Island. I remembered my father. When he left I was a little girl, and he wrote letters and sent money before the war started.

My cousin Harry's first cousin became a matchmaker. They said to my husband (who had immigrated in 1910 and served in the American army in World War I), "This girl is clean-cut and comes from a well-known family. Why don't you marry her?" He was a good husband. We worked together in the export-import business in wholesale groceries. My husband respected me, and I respected him. I like my husband's family.

I am proud to be an Armenian. I try to preserve Armenian customs, art, food. In the past, as a child, I had a miserable life, but when I came to the United States it was like paradise for me. I read and go to all the Armenian meetings and cultural events, and I work hard in the Armenian church in New York. But I love the United States.

VARTAN HAR(OU)TUNIAN, son of a Christian minister and a mother who was a schoolteacher, experienced firsthand the Turks' persecution of the Armenian people. He escaped with his parents, his older brother, and three older sisters in 1922 when he was seven years old.[6]

I was born in 1915 in the city of Marash (Maras). My father was a Protestant minister and had a close relationship with the missionaries from the Congregational Church of America. When he was deported shortly after my birth, my mother and I were kept safe in the American hospital, and my three sisters were kept in the German orphanage.

All I remember was that I was hungry most of the time. My mother had a bag of dried bread and cheese, and whenever I cried for food she would give me a couple of nibbles because there was not enough food even in the American hospital. I didn't know my father until he returned when I was five years old. When I saw him I was afraid of him, because his beard had grown real long and he looked like a man who has just come out of a dungeon. But he had a red apple. I had never seen an apple or an orange before. So I went to him, and it was the first time we embraced as father and son.

When my father came back, we returned to our home in Marash, which had not been destroyed at the time. There was joy and peace and a reunion with the survivors, but it lasted for only a short time (1918–19). Then the whole situation began to change. Turkish troops were ordered to clear out the remaining Armenians, and that's when our tragedy began.

My father had been hopeful when the Armistice was signed and surviving Armenians began to return. But then the troops of Mustafa Kemal began their drive toward the west, and they came into Marash. I was six years old then, hiding in a church that the Turks were trying to set on fire. My father, thinking this was the end of our family, gathered us around him and pulled the movable pews around us, as if he was trying to protect us. He said something I will never forget: "Don't be afraid, my children, because soon we will all be in heaven together." Fortunately, someone discovered some secret tunnels that had been dug from the church to another vantage point, and we escaped.

My father realized that there was no more hope for the Armenians. The American missionaries came to him and said, "We have secret information that they are going to exterminate your family." So that night we were put in an American truck, and we were covered with canvas. About 2:00 a.m., they drove us out of Turkey into Syria, which was under French control at the time. I remember the relief when the canvas was removed so we could breathe, and we crossed the Syrian border in the morning when the sun was just rising. We just had the clothes on our back and a small suitcase.

We were taken to the home of a friend of my father's, and I ate for the first time a meal of spaghetti and ground meat. We stayed there for a while, and then Father wrote to his American friends in the United States. My father received eight hundred dollars with which he paid for the family's passage on a French boat from Aleppo to Smyrna, which was under Greek control at that time. We arrived safely in Smyrna.

After a pleasant three months in Smyrna, tragedy struck again. Mustafa Kemal's troops forced the Greek army into retreat. We were having supper in the basement of our house when we heard our neighbor's screams. A band of Turks had attacked the house next door. My mother opened the basement window, and we all crawled out of the little window and ran to the American compound, which was several blocks away. Several thousand Armenians were taking refuge there, and the compound had the American flag flying over it. While Father was in the front of the main door, one Armenian came and said, "The Americans are leaving from the back." So we just followed the Americans.

I remember the march from the compound to the harbor because many times we had to march between two walls of flames. All the houses had been set on fire. My mother fainted, and my father and brother picked her up. Father took my sisters and me to the shore, where the battleship *Simpson*, anchored there, was taking on Americans. People were jumping in the water, trying to get on the ship. My father ran up to an American acquaintance and said, "Save my children."

And they pushed us into a little boat, and a pulley took the boat to the battleship. Then we had to climb up a rope ladder on the side of the battleship to get on deck. I was only six and half years old. Climbing up this rope suddenly I began to fall backward. I remember praying. To this day I am sure that some angelic being was there to push me back on the rope, and then my sister and I got on deck, crammed with people. Then they also took my mother and father and my other siblings.

That night, my father and I sat on a shelf on the side of the battleship, and we were watching the city burn. If you have never seen a city burning at night, it's like hell, and you hear the people's screams. Some of these experiences and scenes are still with me. After three days at sea we arrived at Piraeus, a refugee camp near the port of Athens. We were given a small room for the entire family, and relief organizations set up by the American government and by Armenians fed us. I remember very vividly when my father came into our little room with a smile on his face and a dish of barbecued lamb in his hands. We each took a little piece, and it was like communion.

We were there three months, and then father got his passports and visa, and we took a third-class passage on the *King Alexander*. It took us twenty-three days to cross the Atlantic, and the stormy weather was beyond our imagination. We thought several times we would sink. The food was mostly macaroni, and everybody was vomiting except me.

We stayed on Ellis Island for several weeks, because my father and mother had problems with their eyes and they had to be in the hospital. We children were separated from our parents. My three sisters and I stayed together. They let me go into the women's quarters because I was the little one, the one who had to be taken care of. Each person got a blanket that smelled of disinfectant, and the cots had blankets that were reasonably comfortable.

The wildness was at the dinner table. We could see these beautifully set long tables with napkins and butter and bread, but as soon as the doors opened, there was bedlam and the butter and bread would disappear. I had my first taste of a banana and a ham sandwich, which I loved. I had never tasted anything so good as a boiled-ham sandwich.

When we left Ellis Island we got on a train to Buffalo, where my mother had a brother who had come years before to America. My mother's name is Shushan, which in Armenian means lily. So we were on this train, and my father says in Armenian to my mother, "Isn't it strange, someone is calling you. Who would know you are here?" And we were puzzled when all of a sudden we see a man coming down the aisle, yelling, "Shoe shine, shoe shine!"

We stayed with my uncle in Buffalo until my father received an invitation to be associate minister of an Armenian church in Philadelphia. So we went there, and that's where my American life really began, in West Philadelphia, Pennsylvania. We changed our name from Haroutunian to Hartunian. It means one who has been resurrected from the dead. "Christos Haroutun (Christ rose from the dead)," we say. And in a sense *we did* rise from the dead.

We call ourselves Armenian Americans. We are 100 percent American. I love this country. I would praise a free and independent Armenia, but I would stay an American. If it weren't for the American missionaries, I wouldn't be here. If it weren't for the freedom of this government, I never would have learned this language. I never would have had this church (in Belmont, Massachusetts). So all of these are very positive factors. The Statue of Liberty and Ellis Island are very meaningful symbols, and they have to be preserved.

The ship *King Alexander* that brought the boy Vartan and his family to New York in 1922 also carried fourteen-year-old JOHN ALABILIKIAN and his aunt to freedom. The Turks had killed John's parents in 1915 when he was seven years old. A Turk who had married his aunt had adopted him and brought him up as a Muslim. This story is how John found his Armenian American identity.[7]

My parents were killed by the Turks in 1915 when they were in their mid-thirties. The Turks took my father away from his business one morning, and they locked him up. The next morning he and five hundred Armenian men were taken out of the city with their arms tied together. Nobody knew where they went, but later on we were told that they had been killed. There were no males left in the town of Yozgat, where I was born—only children, mothers, and grandmothers. Then one morning they did the same thing with the women. They said, "You are gonna be taken out of the city." So we left the city. Many died during their travels.

We stopped at a village that was occupied by Turkish people. There was a bridge there, and four women standing on each side of the bridge told us, "If you want to change your religion, you will be saved. If not, you will be killed." There were nine of us: my mother, myself, my sister and a one-year-old baby in her arms, my mother's sister with her three girls ages nine to about thirteen, and my grandmother. My mother didn't want to change her religion. Then they asked us to drop all the valuables we had in a bag and herded us across the bridge. Someone gave a command to start killing.

We were saved by the partner of my aunt's husband who was one of the organizers of this massacre. When he saw my aunt, he said, "Follow me." My aunt got her three daughters and myself out. My mother, my sister and the little baby, and my grandmother were left in there to die. We came to a little inn where there were twenty to thirty young women who had been taken out by the Turks, and we stayed there for a while with the Turkish man's help. Finally we ended up back in Yozgat, and my aunt married the fellow who saved us and one of her daughters married a Turkish farmer. Then I was circumcised, and a big party was given for me because I had changed my religion.

My aunt sent her unmarried daughters to Constantinople, and I went into a boy's orphanage run by the British. During the three years I was in the orphanage I learned the Armenian language and Armenian history. In 1922 my aunt came to Constantinople, and she, her oldest daughter, and I took a boat, the *King Alexander,* for America. Money for the passage was no problem because my aunt came from a rich Turkish man's house.

When we entered New York Harbor after more than twenty days' travel, the boat blew its whistle and we saw the Statue of Liberty. You are looking at it and you are saying, "Thank God, I am free." The day we arrived I wore a Boy Scout suit and a belt that said in Armenian, "Be educated and educate."

Before we got out of Ellis Island, there were interpreters who helped us with the questions that were asked by the inspectors. My aunt could not read, and the Armenian interpreter said to her, "Take this book and say the Lord's Prayer." And that's what she recited, looking at the book as if she was reading it. We were fortunate that we passed the physical examinations, including the eye exams. The three of us passed without problems. The ship we were on was the last one that came to this country that year. After that the quota system started. We were among the last Armenians to enter this country without too much trouble.

After we left Ellis Island we took a train to Philadelphia, where one of my aunt's daughters lived. Her husband, who had sponsored us, was well-to-do and owned a nice house. He was wheeling and dealing in real estate, and there was quite an Armenian community there. Most of them were relatives who brought other Armenians here.

I learned English in the public school. I went to school for three years. I was too proud to be supported by my sponsor (who wanted me to continue to go to school). I wanted to be an auto mechanic. The man I was working for loved me just the same as he did his children. After working for him for six years, the Depression came. I lost the eight hundred dollars I had in the bank, but I still had twenty-five dollars in my pocket. With that money, I rented a place and set up my own shop. The man I had worked for said, "Anything you want from my shop— my advice, my tools—don't hesitate." That's how much he liked me. Thank God I didn't do too bad. I was in business for about forty years.

When I went to become a naturalized citizen, the last question they will ask you is if you want to change your name. And I did. My aunt was still living, and she had brought me into this country as her son. Her name was Satian. And she said, "I want you to take your own name, your father's name. You are Alabilikian." When I told this story to the immigration officer, he laughed and said, "Most of the people change from a long name to a short name. Now *you* want to change it from the short to the long."

7

German Immigrant Children During the Great Depression

Midway between the opening and closing of Ellis Island, there was a spurt of immigration from economically devastated Germany to the United States. The decade of the 1920s saw a number of German families with children looking for a better life in the United States. Among them were families who had lost their sons or fathers in World War I and their savings in the hyperinflation and Great Depression that followed the end of that war. Others sensed the dangers of the political extremes on the right and the left that threatened to topple the fledgling democratic Weimar Republic and that eventually led to the rise of Adolf Hitler and the Third Reich.

The German currency, the mark, had begun to slide in 1921 and dropped to 75 to the dollar. The next year, it fell to 400, and by the beginning of 1923 to 7,000. The French occupation of Germany's industrial heartland, the Ruhr, strangled the German economy and hastened the mark's final plunge. By November 1923, it took 4 billion marks to buy a dollar. German currency had become worthless on the world market. The life savings of the middle- and working-class people were wiped out; the purchasing power of their salaries and wages was severely restricted. People went hungry and millions lost their jobs.[1]

When the stock market crashed on Wall Street in October 1929, Germany and the United States faced major economic upheavals, requiring their respective governments to take draconian measures. Despite these hardships, the German child immigrants who tell their stories here managed to build satisfying and successful lives in their adopted country.

* * *

INGE NASTKE was ten years old when she traveled with her maternal grandparents to the United States in 1922. Her father had been killed in World War I. Her grandparents hoped to escape the economic and political decline of postwar Germany and try their luck on a ranch in Montana, where her grandmother's sister had settled decades earlier.[2]

> My grandparents actually raised me because my mother was a widow. My father was killed during the war. My mother had to go out and work. She had a very good job in the telegraph office in Hamburg, but there was no one there to take care of me, so my grandparents took over. They had retired and lived in a suburb.
>
> My grandfather was very well known in the fish business, both in Germany and abroad. He imported and exported fish, marinated them, barbecued them, and canned them. He had enough money saved to buy property and a beautiful home. But my grandmother wanted to get away from Germany, because the country was down at rock bottom, economically and politically, and there were constant rumors of an impending civil war.
>
> She had been corresponding with her sister in Montana for years and years, and finally, after a lot of commotion, we boarded a large ocean liner in Hamburg and were ready to go in October 1922. My mother stayed behind in Germany. She said, "I am not going to be destitute when I come to the United States. As soon as I can get some English pounds I will come over."
>
> It took us almost two weeks to cross the Atlantic because we were fighting against terrible gale winds. The ship was shaking and tossing this way and that way. Finally, early one morning nobody was rocking the boat anymore. I quickly got dressed

and sneaked upstairs, and I saw the Statue of Liberty. I thought it was the most beautiful statue I had ever seen, and I have never, ever forgotten it. Pretty soon all the other passengers came up, and they were just flabbergasted to meet "the beautiful lady with the lamp."

We were all interviewed and examined at Ellis Island. While we were waiting I was surprised by a black man who held a tray with all kinds of sandwiches and coffee and tea and milk. He told me to "go ahead," and I had my very first ham and cheese sandwich, which I loved, and a glass of milk. And my grandparents were happy to get a cup of good hot coffee.

After a while they called my grandparents' name. We had to step forward, and the official said to my grandfather, "I am sorry, Mr. Schramm, we cannot release you from Ellis Island. You have passed the age limit; the limit for immigrants is seventy years. You will be detained on this island until your sponsors can produce a five thousand–dollar bond. Your million marks are worthless inflation money." My grandmother, who was very high strung, started to cry. She was heartbroken.

Then an official took us down the hall to a huge room packed with immigrants. So here we sat and were told to wait. I looked at all the people in their fancy costumes, and I thought it was like a masquerade. I was wearing a wool dress, plaid, with long sleeves and velvet cuffs and a velvet collar. I had gloves and a little velvet cap to match my dress. My grandmother had a very lovely wool coat with a fur collar and a velvet hat, and my grandfather had a very nicely tailored overcoat. We were by no means poorly dressed. And so we waited— for nearly two weeks.

My grandfather was always active, in spite of his age. He had to keep moving. So he just wandered around. Finally after a while, he came back to where we were and said, "Come on, let's go over to Germany." He had found a group with whom we were able to converse in our own language, so we could talk and laugh, especially my grandmother.

After I got used to the surroundings, I was bored, and I just walked up to the kids. Some of them talked Russian, some of them Hungarian, and some of them Italian, but it didn't bother us that we were not able to converse in a uniform language. We got together and we chased one another, played hide and seek, and one of the kids had a ball we would throw to this corner and to that corner. We passed the time.

At about 9:00 p.m., every evening, a bell rang, and we had to form a line at the door and then march down to two halls. At the end of one hall, the men had to walk into their separate quarters and the women and children to their quarters. At the entrance, a black man handed out paper towels and little pieces of soap, and everybody was ordered to pick up two blankets.

It was a huge sleeping quarter, made of steel and wire, and the lower bunks were for the adults and the upper bunks for the children. At about 10:00 p.m., the lights went out excepts for a few lights left burning in the washrooms, so we were able to see enough if we had to get up. I slept fitfully the first night, and when I woke up, I saw a cockroach coming from the wash-room. But they had little containers with disinfectants, and this stopped them from crawling up into our beds.

The Ellis Island authorities had contacted my aunt and uncle in Montana, and they said that they were willing to put up the bond, but it would take a little while to get the five thousand dollars. That was a lot of money at that time. Finally came the word that they would furnish the bond, and as soon as we heard the news, they took us upstairs. It was a welcome change be-cause our new quarters were filled with light, and they had an outdoor court where we could exercise in the fresh air. We had a wonderful view of the Statue of Liberty and all the boats go-ing back and forth.

We were there for one day, and I became very ill with a high fever. They put me in the hospital, and when the fever subsided I got the whooping cough and had to stay in the children's ward for about five weeks. The day I was put in the hospital, the five thousand–dollar security bond arrived, and my grandparents had to leave Ellis Island before I was released. Fortunately, they had made a shipboard acquaintance with a German couple who said, "You come and stay with us until you get notified that your granddaughter can be released from the hospital."

Finally, one day between Christmas and New Year's, I was released. I *did* have a Christmas Eve on "Thermometer Row." A

Annie Moore, first immigrant processed at Ellis Island.
National Park Service

Waiting for
inspection,
Ellis Island.
*Library of
Congress*

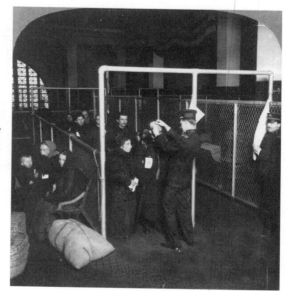

Eye inspections,
Ellis Island.
*Library of
Congress*

Immigrant child and family viewing the Statue of Liberty.
Library of Congress

Children on rooftop garden of main building, Ellis Island. *National Park Service*

Christmas 1905 in the Great Hall, Ellis Island.
National Park Service

First Christmas in America.
Library of Congress

8 Orphan children — Mothers killed in Russian Massacre — Oct. 1905.
SS "Carunia" May 1908

Jewish orphans arrive at Ellis Island, May 1908.
National Park Service

Immigrant children pledging allegiance.
Library of Congress

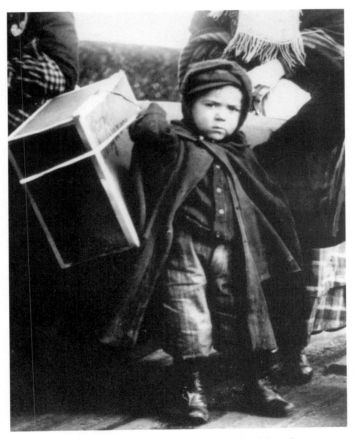

Italian boy, newly arrived at Ellis Island.
National Park Service

Newly arrived mother with three children.
Library of Congress

Immigrant boys with their favorite dog.
Library of Congress

Immigrant children play in the streets of New York. *Library of Congress*

Scandinavian immigrants travel by train to the Midwest.
Library of Congress

Armenian immigrant girl.
National Park Service

Immigrant children being weighed, Ellis Island Hospital.
National Archives

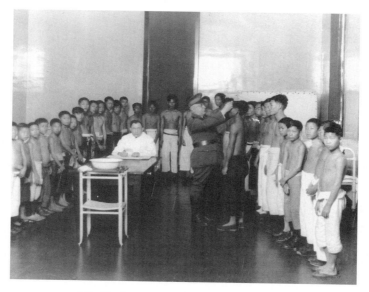

Medical examination, Angel Island.
National Archives

Interrogation,
Angel Island.
*National
Archives*

nurse came on Christmas Eve and brought a little tree, trimmed it, and left me a little package at my bedside. She said, "Fröhliche Weihnachten (Merry Christmas)," and then she was gone. I looked at the package and was overjoyed that someone would think of me. I opened the package, and this very kind nurse had given me a little patent leather handbag and two satin ribbons for my pigtails. And a day after Christmas, another nurse came in and said, "Here are your clothes. Now get dressed, and I'll take you back."

The nurse took me back to the huge waiting room, but there was no grandmother waiting for me. All of a sudden, somebody took me by my arm, whirled me around, and said, "Where in the world did you come from?" It was the matron, the overseer. I explained, "I have just been released from the hospital, and I thought my grandparents were here, waiting for me." She replied, "I am sorry, child, they have been released five weeks ago. Don't cry, we are going to fix you up. Everything will be alright."

My grandparents had taken my winter clothes, my coat, and my hat. I just had my dress, and it was bitter cold. The matron took me down the hall, took one of keys she had around her waist, and opened a door into a room that had a huge pile of clothing, brought there by the Salvation Army, the Goodwill Industries, and the Red Cross. She pulled out a long green wool coat that reached down to my heels, with sleeves that covered by hands; a little gray cap with a red pom-pom, and green mittens.

Then she took me back to the huge vestry hall, and I had to wait there. Somebody came and hung a tag around my neck, and then the official said, "Follow me, you will be brought to Manhattan." So we went down the pier, boarded a little tender, and off we went. As soon as the boat docked at the pier and I went down the gangplank, I saw a Red Cross nurse, and she looked at my tag, and asked, "Du bist Inge (you are Inge)?" I said, "Ja," and she took my hand and replied, "O fine. Come along."

I just put my trust in the nurse. We boarded a streetcar right near the pier and went to the center of town. It was very late in the day, and I was thrilled with the display of electric lights. I just fell over backward, looking at the skyscrapers.

We took another trolley, across town, and then we did a little walking until we reached a long row of brownstone houses on a quiet side street. We walked up the steps of one of these houses, which was a haven for displaced and lost children. Here I spent the night, hoping and praying for a better tomorrow. In the meantime the authorities had notified my grandparents, and on the next day, about 11:00 a.m., they came and brought my regular winter clothing, and we were at long last reunited. It was very emotional. My grandparents and I cried tears of happiness.

And then we set out for Montana and the Wild West. We boarded the train at Penn Station and the trip took us four days. The train made many stops, and I couldn't get over how long we had to travel, all across the land. I kept looking and thought, Where are the Indians? I saw a couple of buffalo but no Indians. I slept on my grandmother's or my grandfather's lap. The conductor was able to speak some German. He said, "Just relax, be comfortable. It'll be a couple of days before we get to Montana." And when we arrived at Great Falls, my uncle was there, wearing a big cowboy hat and a lumber jacket.

His family had immigrated to Montana in 1892 (the year Ellis Island opened up), and my grandmother hadn't seen her sister for thirty long years. When they finally got together, it proved to be a disaster. They couldn't see eye to eye on anything! They were constantly at each other's throats. They fought over the cooking—how to cook this and how to cook that—and at night my grandparents sat on the edge of their beds, their arms around each other, and cried from homesickness.

Conditions were rather primitive. It was just an enormous difference, life on the ranch in Montana and life in Germany. I liked it. I enjoyed it; it was fun. My mother was still in Germany, and it took her a while to get English pounds, because the German mark by now was absolutely worthless. My uncle had already lined up a couple of widowers for her to get married, but my grandfather wrote to her, "Under no circumstances should you come west. Stay in New York, make a little money, and we will join you."

My mother made it to New York after we had been on the

ranch for a year. She was not completely penniless. She went to work as a housekeeper, and she was an excellent cook. My grandparents, on the other hand, were destitute. Their money was gone, but my grandmother still had beautiful earrings, a ring, bracelet, and beautiful diamonds. They sold all her jewelry to buy train tickets back to New York, where my mother was waiting. They worked for two years, saved their money, and then we saw them off on the boat back to Hamburg. Their friends found a little apartment for them.

My mother and I didn't want to go back. My mother always made good money, and I went through high school and then became a student at the White Plains School of Art. I learned a lot there. I did a lot of painting, and I sold a lot. My mother and I were happy staying in the United States.

DORA ESSEL had also lost her father in World War I. She was fifteen years old when she immigrated to the United States and worked in her aunt's bakery in Baltimore. Years later, after the end of War II, she would support her mother and her siblings, who had fled from war-torn East Germany to the West, with CARE packages.[3]

I was born in a small town near Leipzig. My father was killed in action in the first year of World War I. I was six years old, my sister was three, and my brother was three months old. He never saw his father. My mother struggled to support us three children, and when I finished eight years of schooling, I thought, "If I was out of the way my mother would have only two more to support." So I asked my mother's sister, who lived in Baltimore, if they would take me and I would help them in the bakery.

I traveled with two cousins in June 1923, with a big steamer trunk filled with my clothes and school things. We traveled third class, and four of us were in a cabin with bunk beds. There were mostly Germans on the boat. I met a young girl who was only eleven years old; she traveled all by herself to Philadelphia. It took us thirteen days to cross the Atlantic.

At Ellis Island, we were issued a tag with our name on it and our place of destination. We stayed overnight and ate at big tables. Every meal had hard-boiled eggs and bananas. It was on Ellis Island that I saw my first black person; we thought they were Indians. My cousins left after two days with one of the families that sponsored us, and I was left by myself for another twenty-four hours until my aunt Irma came and picked me up. I was not frightened because the people I met would smile at me.

But I was glad to "get home" to Baltimore, because we could not change our clothes during the three days I waited at Ellis Island. I had to help in my aunt's bakery and wait on people and that's how I learned English. I also went to the movies and learned that way. My cousins who spoke only English with me used to call me "Dumb Dora." That name stuck for a while until I spoke the language fluently. My aunt more than once reminded me, "Don't forget: if anything goes wrong, I can send you back to Germany until you are eighteen." So I knew I had to behave. But she was like a second mother to me, and she taught me how to make doughnuts, ice cakes, and bread.

My husband, whom I married in 1933, was German and became a naturalized citizen. When World War II broke out, we were both American citizens already, and no one ever bothered us or my girls in school. My husband was almost drafted. He said, "I don't want to go over there and shoot my own brother or brother-in-law." Luckily he was deferred because he worked in a shipyard. After the war, we sent packages to relatives, to my mother, and to my husband's family.

My mother was still in the East Zone at the end of World War II, but she managed to walk to Berlin in the depth of winter, leaving everything behind. My sister's husband had been transferred to Hamburg. My mother got in touch with my sister and lived with her. I sent money so my sister could go to college, and she got a nice job at the Board of Education afterward. My sister had always wanted to go to college, but my mother's little pension was not enough. Now she visits me a couple of times with her two boys, and my two girls have been over there as well.

My life is better here than if I'd stayed in Germany. I wouldn't trade it for anything in the world. I like it here. Some people complain, but I don't. I am not rich, but I qualify for Social Security. I make out, and that's all I want. My children are happily married, and I've got five grandchildren. Even though my relatives in Germany asked me will I come and live over there, I said, "No way." My roots are here.

EMMI TEGELER KREMER at age nine came to the United States in 1926 and joined her father, who had left Germany three years earlier. Three older siblings, ranging in age from eleven to sixteen years old, and her aunt, who was her guardian in the United States, accompanied her. She now writes poetry, and her "Song of Ellis Island" is on exhibition in the reading room of the Ellis Island Immigration Museum.[4]

I was born in 1917 in the Ruhr area. My father was wounded in World War I. We were occupied by the French after the end of the war, which isolated us from contact with people on the outside. In order to get in and out of town, you had to pass through a barricade with a French guard. My father worked in the coal mines; he was a great speaker and loved politics. He made speeches that were not approved by the political opposition parties, so eventually he had to leave Germany. I remember a group of people coming to our house at night looking for him, and he had already left to join his brother in America.

My mother had died when I was four years old, and I was raised by my maternal grandparents. My grandfather owned a farm, and we lived off the land. We had livestock, and I remember helping him plant potatoes. He would dig a hole and I would drop the potatoes in. He appeared to be very stern, but he was really a very gentle person. My grandmother was a very sweet person, very reserved. Both my grandparents were very religious. My father had been raised Catholic, but he married my mother who was a Protestant. Christmas was strictly for family. Relatives came to visit once a year.

We made our own bread, and our clothes were all homemade and hand-me-downs. For one of my birthdays, grandfather made me a brand-new pair of leather shoes out of an old pair of shoes. We had no radio, no electricity. We had kerosene lamps, and the lights were very low.

One memory I have is of a visit by my aunt, who later became our guardian and brought us to America. She brought chocolate with her. I never had tasted a piece of chocolate. The piece I had dropped to the ground, into the sand, and I picked up the piece of chocolate and wiped it off. It was like precious gold.

Once a year, during harvesttime, all the aunts and uncles would come. They came to help us with the harvesting. It was like a big family reunion, a big celebration. And we children had to sleep in the hayloft upstairs with the mice. Once the hay was harvested, grandfather would bring out his violin, and we would all sit around and sing hymns. And then there was the local beer hall. I have memories of my father going into the beer hall, the *Biergarten*, and of my grandmother getting angry, because she felt that he should be at home instead of politicking.

When my father went to America (in 1923), he right away applied for his citizenship, and after three years he was able to sponsor us [children]. We went to Cologne to get our passports and then by train to Hamburg. We traveled very light. We didn't have much clothing. I missed the animals that had been my companions on the farm. Aunt Frieda, the wife of my father's brother, brought her son along as a traveling companion, so there were six of us in the party. Before climbing the gangplank to the ship, I said to my aunt, "Today is my birthday." She went and bought me an orange. I had never tasted one. With the orange in hand, I boarded the ship. We sailed that same day, March 16, 1926. We traveled third class, steerage, which is all the way at the bottom of the boat.

We climbed down two flights of stairs, and when we got down there, I could hear this rumbling noise from the ship's engine. It stayed with us all through the voyage. We had a small group of musicians on board who traveled around from class to class. They would come a certain night and entertain us. Halfway across the Atlantic we hit a storm, and all the dishes on the table went sliding onto the floor. And the people started falling onto the floor as well, from the ship's rocking back and forth.

People were getting seasick, and they would give us orange juice to drink and pickled herring to suck on to cure the seasickness. I remember going to the bathroom and hearing the rumble of the water below. I couldn't leave the bathroom fast enough because I thought the water was coming up through the toilet. I had seen the fish jumping in the ocean, and I thought the fish were going to jump into the toilet bowl. I was on deck just before the storm started, and a big wave washed over me. Luckily I was strapped in the deck chair; otherwise, the wave would have thrown me right off.

When we landed at Pier 90 in Manhattan, they discovered that I had contracted lice on the ship. A small tender came, took us off the ship, and drove us to Ellis Island. I had to go through a delousing process where they sprayed sulfur fumes all over me. We arrived in the morning, and toward evening we were cleared. They gave us something to eat and drink, and then my father picked us up and took us to Brooklyn.

We lived in a three-story apartment house. My aunt and uncle lived on one floor, and my father had an apartment waiting for us. He had had an accident in the sugar factory where he first worked when he came to the United States, and with the three thousand–dollar settlement he had opened a bakery and a restaurant business. It was right near the docks, and we had all the longshoremen coming in as customers. We had a thriving business.

The day after my arrival I started school at P.S. 30 in Brooklyn, New York, two blocks away from our bakery-restaurant business. I was very proud to be in school, especially on certain days when they had Assembly Days and we had to salute the flag and learn the Pledge of Allegiance. I learned to respect the American flag. So did my father, who joined the Veterans of Foreign Wars (VFW) and wanted to be the carrier of the American flag in the parades.

My father was a very handsome, tall, good-looking man who had no problem attracting women friends. He married twice in the United States. The second marriage that lasted was to Mae West's first cousin. When Mae West was on Broadway, she would send us free tickets. We were financially very secure. Unfortunately, later on, the woman he married wound up with all the money.

I have some very pleasant memories growing up in Brooklyn. When we were growing up, we all had to help in the lunchroom and bakery. At lunchtime, when I went from school to the restaurant, I didn't eat. I had to help wait on the tables. But not far from where we lived there was a library. And I lived in that library. I was always reading.

And I always wanted to write. I remember when I lived in Brooklyn, I used to sit near the docks not too far from Todd Shipyard and Robinson's Shipyard. And I used to look over to the Statue of Liberty, and all of a sudden, a mist would come and cover the statue. I'd sit there by myself and wished that the mist would go away. And then the fog would disappear and I would see the statue again. So when they had the Statue of Liberty celebration I wrote the poem "Sweet Miss Liberty," and I created a melody that would go with the words.

Then I wrote a poem about the American flag, interviewing the people as they came out of the Elmont Library. The American Legion hung "The Star Spangled Banner" poem in their meeting hall, and the Nassau County police, firemen, and state troopers gave me a special award for that poem. And when they began the renovation of Ellis Island, I wrote the "Song of Ellis Island" and composed the music for it at the Elmont Senior Center.

After I had written the words and music, a senior citizen sent my name and the poem to the National Flag Foundation newspaper, and the Veterans of Foreign Wars in Dallas, Texas, asked for my permission to make a bronze plaque with the words of the poem on it. They shipped the plaque to the Ellis Island Library, and now it is at the entrance of a special display room there. I never thought that I would have a poem of mine placed in a national monument. I'd like to share it with everyone who goes there. This is my way of saying "thank you" to America.

I have had so many people along the way help me. There is so much good here in America, if you only look around and reach out. I am still reaching out. I am still trying.

CLARA HONOLD came with her parents and her brother to the United States when she was six years old in 1927, at the height of the Depression in Germany. She worked for the Lutheran church on Staten Island and eventually opened up a progressive school of her own in Florida, serving children from age three to the eighth grade.[5]

I was born in Giengen, a small town near Stuttgart and the Black Forest, famous for the Steiff stuffed animals that are made there. We lived in a three-story home with some fourteen rooms. We had a very spacious living room that was only used for special company and Christmas. There the Christmas tree was set up, and we would enter the room only after supper on Christmas Eve. The tree was already set up, and my father would light the candles. We kept looking out of the window for the Christmas angel and we were asked to perform for her—either sing a song or recite a poem—before we could open our presents. And then we would go to church in a huge sled on Christmas Eve.

Then there was a special parlor with a stove in the corner that radiated a lot of heat. We would sit there in the evenings in a little niche with a round bench, and my father would play the violin and we would sing. And I remember my mother putting apples on top of the stove, and when they were soft and ready to eat, we would all come to the table, and that was our treat. My bedroom was right next to our kitchen, and I spent a lot of time there when I was sick with the chicken pox and other childhood diseases. Being related to the Steiff family, I had a lot of stuffed animals to play with—bears, and lions, and a giraffe with a long neck. If you go into my living room now, you'll see a whole chest with stuffed animals.

The one thing that I remember especially was the kindergarten I attended from age three to age six. The teacher, who was a deaconess, Sister Martha, was a very loving, very wonderful teacher. One day she brought all of us some bananas. It was the first time I had ever tasted a banana. We had our work sack, or knapsack, and everyday we would walk up to the top of a nearby mountain, holding onto a rope with loops on it. And when we would get up to the top of the mountain, we would eat an apple we had brought in our knapsack. To this day, every five years, our kindergarten group meets, and I have been going to their reunion. They keep the stores closed all week for the reunion, so everybody can celebrate.

We left for America because of the Great Depression. My

father was a bookkeeper for Steiff, but they were laying people off, and there was no future for him. The Depression was very severe. That's why Hitler had a chance. Before we left for America, my folks were able to sell our house. We took a large sum of money with us but it didn't last very long, because in 1929 the crash came and we lost every bit of it.

We packed a huge wooden box with our belongings, including a beautiful set of china that my mother had received as a wedding gift and our feather beds. They felt good in New York. I remember a seamstress coming to our house and sewing clothing for me. I had a beautiful wardrobe. And my aunt bought me a brand-new pair of shoes. After a long train ride to Hamburg, we boarded the *Albert Ballin*. It took us ten days to cross the Atlantic.

We had a cabin with three beds. The trip was so stormy that my mother, father, and brother hardly ever got out of bed. But I never got sick. They didn't have the dining room open because it was so stormy, and people just didn't go for their meals. So I was able to go to the chef, and he would give me things to eat. I remember we had to be up very early when we reached New York Harbor. It was dark, and we were at the railing, and it was all so strange and very fascinating. And I remember going to Ellis Island.

My father had a hearing deficiency, and he had to have a physical exam. I remember sitting on a hard bench, and my mother giving my brother and me a bar of chocolate while my father had to go elsewhere. We were afraid that maybe we would be sent back, and seeing all these people waiting was frightening, too. But since his hearing problems was not hereditary, we were allowed to stay. A cousin of my father's met us and took us to Jamaica, which was not very far from the pier where we had landed.

They took us to their home, where we were to occupy the attic. It was quite a shock to us because we had lived very nicely in a large house. It was very uncomfortable, and soon we all began to itch. We found out that there were bedbugs, so we didn't stay very long. We rented a cold-water flat; there was no heat in any of the rooms. The first school I went to was in

Jamaica. I was put in the first grade and I encountered the first black student, a girl who admired the ring I was wearing, removed it, and put it on her own hand. My mother got the ring back from her without saying a word.

It took me about two weeks to interact with my classmates, and then I learned English very quickly. My father first worked in a butcher shop and then in a nursery, transplanting plants. Since he was a bookkeeper and good with figures, he was eventually hired by the Continental Baking Company. My mother took on cleaning jobs.

The first four years in America were very difficult: my brother died from diphtheria, and we lost our savings in the 1929 crash. After leaving the cold-water flat in Jamaica, we went to St. Albans and rented a house there. We had no furniture except beds to sleep in and a chair we had won at a church raffle. The next thing that went into our living room was a piano, and then I started taking violin lessons. I remember the home we did get to own. It had been foreclosed but was completely redone—everything was repainted—and it was priced at four thousand dollars. All my mother had in her pocket when she saw the "For Sale" sign was a ten-dollar bill, and that's what it took as a down payment to hold the house. That was the beginning of a change for the better.

My father and mother became citizens very quickly. It was a big event. We had a big dinner for all the people we knew. We didn't even have enough plates for all the friends my mother invited. One of the customs we kept is that we celebrated and exchanged our gifts on Christmas Eve rather than on Christmas morning as is the custom in America. We joined the Lutheran church, and later I went to work for them as a parish worker on Staten Island and on Long Island. Then we moved to Florida. My parents decided they wanted a warmer climate.

I went into real estate and acquired my first property for my first school, which grew tremendously. I acquired more property and built up my school so that I started with three-year-olds and went up to the eighth grade. In the early years I gave to the children what I had had in kindergarten, and people were pleased with my philosophy and the way I handled the children. I think children must experience happiness and security and structure in their early years that will stay with them for life.

I retired two years ago, but now a group of my former parents who had children in my school are meeting to reestablish my school at another location. It is so exciting for me to see the new school materialize. It will be on a farm, and I have always felt that animals and children belong together. It is so thrilling that all these professional people and their wives who had their children with me want to have this school perpetuated for other children in town.

When I could, I had patriotic programs at my school. My children know the national anthem and all the other songs that are patriotic. I am very American, but I cannot overlook the fact that I had such a marvelous heritage. I must share this with others and pass it on.

8

Escape from Hitler's Third Reich

In 1933, at the time Hitler rose to power, some 550,000 Jews lived in Germany. Five years later when Austria became part of Grossdeutschland (Greater Germany), an additional 190,000 Jews came under the National Socialist sphere of influence. Eventually some 130,000 German-speaking Jews made a new home in the United States, with the majority having emigrated in 1938 and 1939.[1]

The government-sponsored persecution of the Jews began already in the first year of the Third Reich, when Jews were excluded from jobs in public office, the civil service, journalism, the theater, the movie industry, radio, and education. Two years later, on September 15, 1935, the Nuremberg Laws deprived them of German citizenship and forbade marriage and extramarital relationships between Jews and Aryans. By 1938, Jews were removed from practicing the professions of law and medicine.

On November 10, 1938, fueled by a Nazi-organized demonstration after a Jewish teenager assassinated a German diplomat in Paris, a night of horror descended on the Jews. During the Kristallnacht (night of the broken glass), Jewish homes, shops, and synagogues went up in flames. The pogroms of November 1938 opened the eyes of those Jews who had hesitated to emigrate. For many a last-minute hunt for necessary papers began. Desperate people pleaded in front of consulate officials for entry visas, and the sale of worthless tickets by unscrupulous profiteers flourished.[2]

Among the first child evacuees from Grossdeutschland were some 10,000 unaccompanied Jewish children who went to England between December 2, 1938, and September 1, 1939, which marked the beginning of World War II in Europe. In an act of mercy, not equaled anywhere else in the world at that time, the British government offered entry visas to children, ranging in age from three months to seventeen years, who were fully, half, or even a quarter Jewish.

Operation Kindertransport was a voluntary effort, spearheaded by Jews and the Quakers, who placed the nearly destitute youngsters in hastily established hostels, schools, and private homes across Great Britain. The effort saved thousands of youngsters from political persecution. Fifty years later, in 1990, some 250 child survivors told their stories in *I Came Alone: The Stories of the Kindertransports*, a collection of memoirs that pay tribute to their parents, who let them go to safety, and to their British hosts' generosity.[3] The children were supposed to find a temporary home while they hoped for reunion with their parents. Nine out of ten children did so in vain. Their parents perished.

One thousand unaccompanied Jewish children came eventually to the United States, sponsored by the National Council of Jewish Women and the Quakers.[4] Here are the voices of four survivors who passed through Ellis Island and were united with their parents.

* * *

HARRY HOCHSTADT came in 1938 as a thirteen-year-old to the United States. Born in Vienna, he was the only child of a Jewish accountant of modest means.[5]

> Austria was primarily a Catholic country, but there was a substantial presence of Jews. Vienna had a population of about two million, and 10 percent were Jewish. On the block that I hung around all the kids were non-Jewish, but we got along. I read a lot; we would go to a lending library. And I enjoyed the movies and the theater matinees. At ten, I passed the entrance exam for the gymnasium.

The Depression hit us hard, and my father was out of work for two years. My father didn't have money to buy me clothing, so a lot of the stuff I wore was cast-offs from my uncle. In 1935 and 1936 we spent the summers in Romania with my parents' relatives, who fed us well. In 1936 my father got a job in Paris, and in 1937 the company assigned him to their Shanghai office. My mother and I were to join him there, but then the war broke out between China and Japan. In March 1938, the Austrians were overrun by the Germans, or the Germans were received with open arms by the Austrians, depending on your point of view!

My recollection is, the Austrians were very happy. Vienna was transformed: swastika flags all over, storm troopers running through the streets, and jubilation. So my mother and I were trapped, and my father was in Shanghai. The schools were closed, and Jews were not allowed to go anyplace. So that meant that all the things I used to do, like going to the movies once in a while or to the park—everything—was closed to Jews.

Eventually the schools were reopened, but now the ground floor in my school was the Jewish floor and the top floors were the Aryan floors. Now when we left school, very often there would be a cordon where we would have to fight our way out of school. The Aryan kids would line up and wouldn't let us through. But there were exceptions: my English teacher, after the schools reopened, came into class in a storm trooper's uniform. He said, "The change in the political regime will not affect us in this classroom," and he meant it. He was a decent man.

So people said, "That's just a lot of noise." My aunt's husband said, "Ahh, you'll see, things are going to calm down, and after a while it will be business as usual." But we, my mother and I, realized we would have to get out. The idea was to apply for visas all over, so at the age of thirteen I became an expert on visas. I could tell you about every country. But my father was still in China and was told he had to go to New York, and he was back in Paris on his way to America in August 1938. My father went to a French diplomat who had married one of my cousins and said, "Please help me get my family out of Vienna." The diplomat called a friend who was the American representative to the Vatican. That man, in turn, called the American ambassador in Vienna. We got a visitor's visa that got us out. Now we still had to get a visa to travel through Switzerland and France, but with the American visa that was no problem. We still had to do a lot of paperwork and obtain a statement from the police that we had no criminal record.

We took clothing and a few books, a couple of suitcases, and each of us were allowed to take ten marks per person. At the Swiss-Austrian border, they took my mother off the train, undressed her, and did a body search to see whether she had any diamonds or jewels hidden on her body. We finally got to Paris and had a great reunion with my father. We stayed there for two months. Then we took the train to Cherbourg to embark on the *Queen Mary*.

We got to New York Harbor on December 1, 1938, but before we even landed a tender came out with customs people on it for an initial screening, and that's when our troubles began. The immigration people examined our papers and found something irregular. They took us to Ellis Island. I was extremely worried because we had no place else but America to go to at this point, and I remember my terrible concern over our future.

In the evening they gave us a meal in the Great Hall, and they served us fish stew. I never liked fish stew, so I just ate bread and butter. Then we had to go to bed in the gallery above the Great Hall. There were little bedrooms, and I slept on a bare bunk with a pillow. I never even undressed. I didn't sleep much because of the terrible concern I had.

The next morning my father managed to reach his official supervisor in the New York office who convinced the authorities that my father's job was for real. We were taken from Ellis Island by a ferry, and my mother's brother, who had been in America for many years, and my father's supervisor met us. We all felt very relieved. We stayed briefly with my uncle, his wife, and their children in their three-room apartment. Eventually we found an apartment in the East Bronx.

My father still worked for a year, closing the books for his company. His office was just across from the public library. I enrolled in the Bronx High School of Science, which was a wonderful school. I just got a news bulletin for the alumni from my high school, announcing that a fifth alumnus has won a Nobel Prize. That's the kind of school it was.

I learned English very quickly, but my father never did. At the end of 1939 when his job ended, about a year after we came, he had a nervous breakdown. He said, "As a Jew, as somebody who doesn't know the American accounting system and not knowing English, I'll never get a job here, so the only thing to do is to go back to Austria." Eventually my father just sat at home, smoked, didn't even get dressed, totally depressed. We were on food stamps for a while, and then my mother took a job in a factory.

I became an excellent student, but when I graduated in 1943, I had to register for the draft. I took a four-day entrance exam to the engineering school in City College [of New York], but I was drafted weeks later. I took my army physical in November and was inducted on December 7, 1943. They needed engineers, but I wound up in the infantry and fought in France and Germany. I was discharged in July 1945 with a Bronze Star.

I decided to go to Cooper Union, a private first-rate engineering school, and graduated in 1949 in chemical engineering near the top of my class. Then I got fellowship at NYU [New York University] to go into a doctoral program in mathematics. I got my Ph.D. officially on February 27, 1956, the day my daughter was born. In 1957 I got a job as assistant professor at the Polytechnic Institute in Brooklyn. I became a full professor in a few years, published several professional books on mathematics, and retired in 1991. I still read a good bit of mathematics, but I also read a lot of history.

In many ways I feel so Americanized that often I don't even think about having come from Austria. But the Hitler period was a really seminal event that will always be with me in a powerful way. I could never, ever consider going back to Vienna. Being in America is great. This is my home, and this is where I belong.

LIESEL RUBIN SARETZKY was born in 1925 in Vienna and experienced the events surrounding the *Anschluss* (union) of Austria and Germany and the Austrian Jews' subsequent persecution that culminated in the Kristallnacht in November 1938. A Kindertransport sponsored by the Quakers and British Jews brought her to temporary

safety in England. She left from Liverpool in 1939 to join relatives
in the United States.[6]

I had a brother who was five years older, and we were brought
up by two loving parents who had a little meat stand in the
Gross-Market in Vienna. My parents were not religious, and
we always had a Christmas tree. My mother and father were
"real Austrians." My father was the head of the local football
team, which consisted of all Christian guys, and when Hitler
came to Vienna, my father used to say," Ah, this can't be." He
was in total denial. We led a very simple life, and when he
couldn't go to work anymore, we still managed to have a little
Cream of Wheat for supper.

Then they told us we had to go to a Jewish school. The
Hitler Youth boys would be ready outside to spit at us, and
they would say, "Give us a *groschen* (penny), and we won't spit
on you." So in the morning my mother would give me a few
pennies so the boys won't spit on me. When my brother turned
eighteen, they took him and other eighteen-year-old boys to
the Police Academy, which was just across from our building
and had become a Gestapo headquarters. My father's brother
had a Catholic wife who was tall and beautiful and was an
American citizen. She was visiting Vienna at the time. Wearing
a pin with the American flag, she went to the Police Academy,
marched my brother out of jail, provided him with exit papers,
and took him right to the train and onto a ship that sailed to
America.

On Kristallnacht, November 10, 1938, the synagogue across
the street from where we lived was totally destroyed. We all
collected ourselves in one Jewish apartment in our building; it
was like wall-to-wall Jews in that apartment. In a million years
I didn't think I would survive. But I did what my rabbi said:
"Stay inside of your heart, and it's beautiful in there. People
out there are ugly and horrible, but God lives inside and is with
us, no matter what. People have free will to be horrible, but
people have also free will to be good."

After my brother left for America, they were still schlepping
Jews every day across the street to the police headquarters. We
had a woman upstairs who was a single "old maid" lady who

lived with her brother. The brother became an instant Nazi in a black (SS) outfit. My rabbi lived one floor below us, and they dragged him down six floors. He kept falling, and they picked him up by his beard. And the woman would stand there and clap, "Good, good, another Jew is gone." And she used to come and eat in our house!

I used to think, Why isn't somebody saving us? There must be people who know this is going on. Where are they? In my case the Kindertransport came and I was helped. There were Quakers in England who decided to save the Jewish children, and my father found out about them. My aunt in London, who was quite poor, signed all the papers and found a foster family for me. Within a couple of weeks my father got the papers for me to go with a Kindertransport. The next thing I know I am sitting on a train with hundreds of children—little babies, three-year-olds, ten-year-olds, and myself. We had to be quiet. You could hear a pin drop. When the train left, I remember my mother looked shabby, my father looked skinny, but we didn't wave. We didn't cry. We became like stones. Nobody talked.

We went through Holland, which was not yet occupied, and it was the first time that I saw human kindness. The Dutch women ran when they knew the train was coming, and they had milk and cookies. They couldn't wait to give them to us with a napkin, and they kissed us. I felt so good. And then I came to London. This family with two girls younger than I took me in, and we became close. I stayed with them for nine months.

I didn't speak any English, but they spoke Yiddish, so they could understand German. I went to school, and the children brought me presents. They were wonderful. I was a smart girl, and I learned English very fast and learned poetry. School was my cup of tea. But I was lonely and miserable, and I slept with my parents' and my brother's picture under the pillow. I tried to find out about my parents, but their letters came through the Red Cross and I didn't hear. I was totally miserable. I just wanted to come to America, where my brother worked in a factory in Boston. I loved the Tishes, but I knew that B'nai B'rith, the Jewish organization, gave them money to keep me, and that made me feel bad. They gave me a few shillings, and every Sunday I went to visit my aunt. I adored her.

I heard from my brother. I was in constant touch with him. After nine months, through my brother and another uncle, I came up with the money for the passage from London to New York. And Mr. Tish belonged to a synagogue, and he brought me there one Saturday morning. And he asked them all, "Look at this beautiful girl. Now we are going to pass the hat for money." We collected enough for the journey, and they gave me a golden mezuzah. When I left school, the children gave me a party. I had a suitcase and all my papers, and I went on this Dutch boat by myself. I was seasick all the time.

The day before we arrived in New York, my uncle and my brother had come down from Boston to pick me up. In the morning a motorboat came alongside our ship, and we were heading for Ellis Island. It was like a prison, I thought at the time. We ate in a big dining room and slept in a huge dormitory, and if we had to go to the bathroom, a matron came with you with a key. In the morning my uncle was waiting for me and took me on a subway to his home. It was the Garden of Eden for me. And then after a week or two they gave me money to go to Boston and be with my brother. Soon after that my mother came, with the help of an uncle in New York who was able to get affidavits for her.

My father was still in Vienna. A roommate of my brother's was an engineer. He loaned five thousand dollars to my mother—you needed that amount of money in the bank to show that a refugee would not be a burden to the United States—and that opened the door for my father to leave Austria. So he arrived in Boston, we came to pick him up, and then we all lived together in a little apartment. The Salvation Army gave us the furniture. The Jewish committee came every month and paid our rent, but we soon became independent. My mother washed floors, and I helped her after school, always a little embarrassed. But we worked and we didn't take charity.

I was very good in high school. Reading books and getting As was my forte. So my mother said, "You have to go to college. You can't work in the factory. You are too smart and I want you to have a better life." So I went to Simmons College, which is a very fine girls' school, and I studied nutrition and became a dietician. For a refugee girl at that time to go to college was a huge achievement.

And I made it out of poverty. My first husband was a physician. We had a beautiful house, two cars, three fabulous kids, a maid. But slowly, slowly, like the Nazis, alcohol became an obsession for me. And then my husband got cancer and died. I was a woman in my early forties with three young children: nine, fifteen, and eighteen years old. I drank. I worked, but I had hangovers. I joined AA [Alcoholics Anonymous] and have been sober for thirty-five years.

My oldest daughter, who has a Ph.D., also drank. She was having nightmares about the Holocaust. When she finally got sober, she felt she had to go to Auschwitz, and we went. The prayer we said there for those who were killed was, "We didn't forget you, and we are here to tell you that God picked us to go on and we are living instead of you, but we are trying to make the world better." Rather than just feel guilty, I now give thanks for living. I think if God gave me talents, I have to use them. So I wrote a story for a book called *I Came Alone* about the Kindertransports.

Now we have reunions of those who were in the Kindertransports in New York and Florida, and every three years we have a huge reunion from all over the world. The last one was in London. From the reunions I have met a whole world of Kinder—the ones who lost their parents—but they don't have the guilt. They gave their pound of flesh. I don't know why so many others died, and I was picked out to live. All I know is that if God decided that I should live, then every day I should strive to make the world a little better. So I make quilts for the Make-A-Wish Foundation and volunteer with underprivileged African American children.

ARNO PENZIAS, born into a middle-class Jewish family in Munich, arrived in New York in January 1940 at age seven. He and his younger brother had been sent with a Kindertransport to England in the spring of 1939 to escape Nazi persecution. Penzias became a radio astronomer at the Bell Laboratories in New Jersey. In 1978 he shared the Nobel Prize in Physics for the discovery of cosmic microwave background radiation, which lent empirical support to the big bang theory of the creation of the universe.[7]

I spent the first six years of my life comfortably in a closely knit family. Even when my family was rounded up for deportation to Poland it didn't occur to me that anything bad could happen to us. After some days of back-and-forth on the train, we were returned to Munich. I learned that everything would be fine if we could get to "America."

In the late spring of 1939, shortly after my sixth birthday, my parents put their two boys on a train (that connected with a Kindertransport) to England. We each had a suitcase with our initials painted on it, as well as a bag of candy. They told me to be sure to take care of my younger brother Günther. I remember telling him, "Jetzt sind wir allein (now we are alone)," as the train pulled out.

My mother received her exit permit just a few weeks before the war broke out and was able to join us in England. My father had arrived in England almost as soon as the two of us, but we hadn't seen him because he was interned in a camp for alien men. We spent six months in England awaiting passage to America and sailed at the end of December 1939. The gray three-inch gun on the aft deck was a great attraction for us boys.

We arrived in New York in January 1940. My brother and I started school in the Bronx, and my parents looked for work. They became "supers," or superintendents of an apartment building. Our basement apartment was rent-free, and it meant that our family would have a much-needed second income without my mother having to leave us alone at home. As we got older, my mother got a sewing job in a coat factory, and my father's woodworking skills helped him land a job in the carpentry shop of the Metropolitan Museum of Art.

It was taken for granted that I would go to college. "College" meant the City College of New York, then beginning its second century of moving the children of New York's immigrant poor into the American middle class. I discovered physics in my freshman year. Graduation, marriage, and two years in the U.S. Army Signal Corps saw me applying to Columbia University in 1956. My army experience helped me get a research assistantship in the Columbia Radiation Laboratory, then heavily involved in microwave physics.

In 1961, with my Ph.D. thesis complete, I went in search of a job at Bell Laboratories in New Jersey. I remained there for more than thirty years. I made it my business to engage in the communications work at Bell Labs in addition to my work as a radio astronomer. In 1972 I became the head of the Radio Physics Research Department and a visiting member of the Astrophysical Sciences Department at Princeton University. I felt that I learned far more from my students than I could possibly have taught them.

FRED CIGE reached Ellis Island in September 1941, one month shy of his twelfth birthday. His younger brother, Sigmund, accompanied him. The boys were refugees who had come from a children's home in southern France, after having escaped their native Berlin in December 1938. They had spent time in Brussels, Belgium, in 1939 and then in the unoccupied part of France in 1940 and 1941 until the Children's Aid Society (Oeuvre de Secours aux Enfants [OSE]) sponsored their passage to the United States.[8]

I was born in Berlin on October 31, 1929, in an upper middle-class family. My parents had established a very good life. My father was a tailor who employed about ten people. After Hitler came to power, things changed dramatically. When I got to be six years old, I became quite aware of the fact that we were Jewish. There were signs all over that read *"Juden Verboten"* (Jews forbidden) on park benches, so we could not sit there. My father was hauled before the Gestapo because a Jew was not supposed to tell Aryan people who worked for him how to behave. I learned very early that I had to be very careful of what I said and did.

My parents came from religious families and went to the synagogue on major holidays. Our food was kosher, and the school I went to was a public school but only for Jewish children. One day we were taken to the courtyard of the school and all the books that were in that school were thrown into a pile and burned by the Germans.

We played outside and there were children who belonged to the Hitler Youth. They were like Boy Scouts—they wore little short pants and uniforms—except that they wore daggers. One day about three of them started chasing me, which was a fearful experience. And I saw stores smashed in during Kristallnacht, the night of broken glass, November 9–10, 1938.

Shortly after that my parents decided to leave. The family went in three phases. My father and I escaped first from Germany into Belgium. I was nine years old at the time, in December 1938. My brother, who was eight, and my sister, who was one, were the only ones who came into Belgium legally. My mother put them on the train to be met in Brussels by my father. And then my mother escaped, and we were reunited in Belgium. My parents had left most things we owned behind.

My father and I left Berlin by train and wound up in Cologne. From there, my father and I took a train to Aachen. From Aachen we were transported to the Belgian border. My father and I were examined at the border station. They took all the money he had away from him, except for the ten marks they said he could keep. I'll never forget there was a guard there and he had a gun with a bayonet on it. I guess, for fun, he pointed it at my father's stomach and then pointed it at my stomach.

My father was told to spend the marks at a food place across from the guard house, and we went in there briefly, and then came out and went around to where there was a barbed-wire fence. My father helped push me over, then climbed over himself. Then we walked around in the no-man's land until we were met by two men, smugglers whom my father had hired. They decided that the two [of] us should be separated. The one who took my father spoke German and did all the talking. The one I went with did not, and I was afraid I would not see my father again. Eventually we came to a house where there was a truck. My father was already there.

We were driven to Brussels, where we were taken to a house where other illegal immigrants stayed. We lived for a while in the attic, then my father found a small apartment over a butcher shop. He worked as tailor to support us. Then my parents arranged for my mother to put my brother and sister on the train to come from Germany to Belgium. The two were going by themselves. My eight-year-old brother was in charge of watching his baby sister. There was a woman who took the two kids under her wing, and in the last minute my father found them at the station in Brussels before the train was going on to Antwerp.

And then my mother left Germany illegally for Belgium. She had the most difficult time with the smugglers; they made off with the jewelry she had brought across the border. But we were eventually reunited in Brussels, and my father made ends meet with tailoring. I became the interpreter because I picked up French faster than my parents.

Life was not nearly as luxurious as we had in Germany, but I began to relax a bit and live the life of a nine-year-old boy. I attended a public school, but there were a lot of Christian symbols and holiday celebrations, so it was almost as if I was attending a Catholic school. Then one night, in the spring of 1940, the sky was full of German planes. And they started bombing the city and there were explosions all over. The Germans were invading Belgium.

So we took whatever belongings we could carry and headed for the Gare du Nord [North Train Station]. We eventually wound up in the freight car of a train that took us into France, and we ended up in a tent city in Ravel. We lived in this settlement for about a month. It was not bad for us children, because we ran around outdoors and we took long walks and visited the vineyards. One day we were rounded up and taken on a train to Adga, one of the concentration camps in Southern France. It was not a camp like Auschwitz or Bergen-Belsen— there were no gas chambers or systematic killing—but life there was very hard. They were work camps. The men were in separate sections from the women and children, and there were gypsies as well in a separate section.

On a typical day we boys played games together, but we were well aware of the fact that there were guards and we were surrounded by barbed wire. Several times we escaped. We dug holes underneath the fence, and we were small enough so we could crawl through these holes. Then we put cardboard on top of these holes so you couldn't tell that they were there. That was toward the back of the camps where guards were very seldom seen, or they just ignored us. We wound our way into Adga. In town we didn't have any problems, because we spoke French. When we had money we brought back some food for our parents, and there were times when we stole some things from the market.

The women and children lived in military barracks from World War I, and we had straw on the ground that we could sleep on. The men slept on hard wood. They brought food in on trucks, and you lined up. Most of the time it turned out to be turnips. One day we were thrilled we had some meat in the soup, but we all ended up with food poisoning. And so there was a lot of feces all over the place. There wasn't much you could do.

One day a woman came to the camp. My parents had apparently agreed that my brother and I would go with her, and she would take us to where we'd be safe and things would be better for us. Then she brought us to this children's home with my parents' approval. It was called Chateau de Masgelier. And we found other children there. One of the reasons that my brother and I were chosen, we were told, was because we were sick. I had stomach problems, and my brother had lung problems. When we got there, I ended up in the infirmary. I was given zwieback and other little goodies.

The home was a healthy environment for us. I had never known about showers before; they had showers there. We said a little prayer before we ate and before we went to sleep. Every night we were told a story. The one I vividly remember is *Les Misérables*. We could relate to the people in that story because the hero is a man who is being hunted down for having stolen a piece of bread, and we had been hunted down a good part of our lives. We wrote to our parents, and they wrote to us from the work camps. We were there about nine months when my parents showed up, having received a laissez-passer, a document that allowed them to travel from the camp to the children's home.

My parents sat down with us in the children's home and told us that they had given approval for us boys to go to the United States. Then they turned to me and said that I should take care of my brother, who was one year younger than I, and told him that he had to listen to me, which created some difficulties. We were brought together with children from other children's homes, and fifty-one of us were taken to Marseilles, where we stayed for a month and then left for Lisbon. There we boarded the *Serpa Pinta*. We were taken care of by American Quakers. I have a lot of respect for them because they helped Jewish children escape and they didn't ask anything for it. Their intent was not to convert anybody to their faith but simply to save some Jewish children.

The voyage was interesting. The ship was a freighter, loaded with cork. It did have places for us to sleep, but these were not luxury accommodations. We went first to Casablanca in North Africa, where we stayed one night, and then we were on the ocean for ten days, watching the dolphins at the front of the boat. Then we stopped in Bermuda for two days, and then we were cleared by the British for the journey to New York. The most memorable emotional experience for me was seeing the Statue of Liberty. That giant statue inspired all of us at the guardrail to look at her. The sight was overwhelming. But then the doctors who boarded the ship and examined us took me to Ellis Island because I had stomach problems and high fever. I stayed at the hospital for a week. I was the only one taken from the ship, and my biggest concern was that I might be sent back to Europe.

In the hospital I was in a strange place in a strange land, and I didn't understand the language. They put me on a cot, and there was a man who befriended me and took care of me. He made me feel comfortable and reassured me that I would be OK. He gave me my first American coin—a quarter—that I kept for a long time. After I week I was taken from Ellis Island to Manhattan with its giant buildings and then to a children's home in Pleasantville in upstate New York, where I was reunited with my brother.

After about a month my brother and I were separated from the other kids and sent on a long train ride to St. Louis, where we were under the charge of a Jewish children's society at the local children's home. I spent the first week in a hospital with a diagnosis of "nervous stomach." Then my brother and I were placed in our first full-time foster home with the Wolff family. We were treated beautifully there. The man had served in the war and spoke German, which was very helpful. They had one son, and they were just very good to us. They opened the world for us. But after a year and half, my brother developed serious emotional problems, so we were put in separate foster families. We were moved several times, separately, to new foster families. The fifth foster family, the Zemlicks, was very good, and my brother and I were together again.

I was trying to catch up with my education. I had missed what amounted to six years of education. I took the fifth and sixth grades at the same time and went to summer school, and I managed to graduate from high school. But my brother, by the time he was in the eleventh grade, quit school and joined the army. Meanwhile, my parents had gotten to Switzerland, and through distant relatives who lived in Queens, they managed to come to this country. I saw them after ten years, when I was twenty-one years old and already an American citizen. The sister I had left at age three was now thirteen years old, and now there were also eight-year-old twin sisters whom I had never seen.

My brother and I came up from St. Louis, first to visit them and then to live with them in Brooklyn. In St. Louis I had had several jobs in furniture stores and had gone to a community college. In Brooklyn I worked for a furniture store by day and registered at Brooklyn College at night. They didn't charge any tuition except for books, and I maintained a B+ average, working during the day and going to college at night. My father got a job as a tailor.

I majored in English because I fell in love with the language. I spoke German and French, but I loved English literature. It took me eight years to get my BA. By the time I graduated (in 1960), I was married and already had one child. Then I got a master's degree in finance, which took me six years. I didn't finish my education until I was thirty-six years old, by which time I had two children.

After all the experiences I have had, I've come out with a degree of normalcy; I say this because my brother had lots of difficulties. My bother never got married; he could not maintain any lasting social relationships. I am very lucky that I have enjoyed the good fortunes that came my way.

9

Europe's Displaced Children Come to the United States

In the summer of 1945, after World War II had ended, millions of displaced persons (DPs)—refugees, deportees, political prisoners, concentration camp survivors, and forced laborers—were on the move. Most ended up in camps the Allied forces set up in Germany, Austria, and Italy. The DPs had become a stateless people. Among the 1.8 million displaced persons crowded in DP camps by the fall of 1945, 25 percent were children. Many were natives of the Ukraine, of the eastern part of Poland, and the Baltic states—Estonia, Latvia, and Lithuania—regions that had been forcibly incorporated into the Soviet Union. Others were Jewish children who had survived the war or had been born in the camps.[1]

The most pressing concern in the DP camps was to provide food, water, shelter, and sanitation. The next order of business was to open schools. School became a reliable anchor for the displaced children. In every camp, national groups organized their own curriculum, so that the children could catch up with what they had missed during their wartime wanderings. From humble beginnings, despite shortages of textbooks and materials, emerged elaborate camp school systems, extending from kindergarten to high school.

The schools were great equalizers: the children of former

landowners and lowly tenants studied together. In the same classroom were children of Catholic, Orthodox, and Protestant faiths. By the spring of 1946, 90 percent of the DP children, ages five through sixteen years, in the American Zone were attending camp schools, and many adults were enrolled in evening classes.

Meanwhile, more and more Americans began to realize that Europe's refugee problem could not be solved without massive immigration into the United States. In the fall of 1946, a Citizens Committee on Displaced Persons (CCDP) was created. Among its prominent sponsors was Eleanor Roosevelt. President Harry S. Truman, in his State of the Union message in January 1947, called on Congress to authorize a massive influx of DPs.

Opponents delayed the DP bill's passage until the spring of 1948. Truman signed the first DP Act on June 25, 1948, to allow resettlement for 200,000 DPs in the United States over the next two years, and the second DP Act on June 16, 1950, extending the final deadline for issuing visas to December 31, 1951. The American program's crucial feature was the "assurance," a promise from an American sponsor that a displaced person would be provided housing for his family and employment after careful background screening.

In addition to organizations linked to national associations, representatives from Roman Catholic, Lutheran, and Jewish groups became advocates for the DPs. Especially active was the Lutheran World Federation. Eventually, out of more than a million of the war's refugees, nearly 400,000 DPs settled in the United States.

Among the first to land in their new country were some 98 displaced children younger than ten years of age. Ten days out of Hamburg, they arrived in New York on December 21, 1948, aboard the SS *Marine Flasher.* On the afternoon of their arrival, they were guests at a special Christmas party on Pier 62, an event the youngsters remembered with much delight. Those who were young in the camps usually held on to happier memories more than their elders did.[2]

* * *

One of the youngest displaced children to immigrate to the United States was ESTHER BLATT, who arrived in New York on the troopship *General Greenley* in December 1949. The daughter of Jewish concentration camp survivors from Poland, she was three and a half years old.[3]

I was born on May 25, 1946, in Feldafing, a displaced persons' camp south of Munich. My parents married young: my mother was seventeen and my father was nineteen. They were separated after the Nazis invaded Poland. My father was later liberated from the concentration camp Theresienstadt and my mother from Bergen-Belsen. When the war ended, they miraculously found each other with the help of the Red Cross.

We lived in Feldafing until I was three and a half years old. The Americans were in charge of the camp, which meant it was a wonderful place. My father had a job, driving a truck for the American army; we had a pretty place to live in; and we had lots of food.

My parents put in papers to come to America. They came with the sponsorship of the United Jewish Appeal (UJA) and the Hebrew Immigrant Aid Society (HIAS). We have good memories of the things they did for us. We left from Naples, Italy, on an American troop carrier that had been converted to bring immigrants from Europe to the United States. They put the men in the enlisted men's quarters, where they all slept in bunks. The women had what must have been converted officers quarters, which we shared with another woman and her child.

My mother was sick from the moment we got on the ship until we got off. I was sick as well, and at the end of the trip my mother realized that I was getting hotter and hotter and that I needed medicine. She finally told somebody that I was sick, and they took us by ferry to Ellis Island, where there was a hospital. I was separated from her—she stayed in another building—and it was a trying time for her because she was very nervous about everything. When she came to my hospital room she pulled all the shades down because she thought if you had measles (which I had) I needed to be in the dark. The nurses would come and lift the shades, and she would pull them down again, so they were always shooing her away.

And when they brought the trays in for the children and there was a dish of ice cream for me, my mother panicked and grabbed it off the tray. She thought that if you were sick and had a fever, you should have warm things to eat. She couldn't think of any way to dispose of the ice cream, so she gobbled it up very quickly. The nurse saw it and yelled at her. I stayed in the hospital for about a week before we joined my father and a friend from the DP camp who had been brought to the United States by an aunt who sponsored him.

My father hooked up right away with the United Jewish Appeal, and they found us a room in a hotel through the Hebrew Immigrant Aid Society. Every day they took my father to help him find a job and gave bus fare to my mother, so she could go from the hotel to the main office of the HIAS where she could spend the day. My father was a carpenter by trade, so after he found a job, he worked all day as a carpenter and took night courses in English and draftsmanship at the Brooklyn Technical High School. He was always willing to take a chance. He was the first among his friends to get a driver's license. He was confident and curiously optimistic, considering all he had gone through.

We moved to our first apartment in Brooklyn, where we lived on the fourth floor of a tenement building. Everyone in the five apartments on each floor left their doors open, and everyone took my parents in. One woman took my mother to the market and showed her how to negotiate the stores; others explained to her how to use money. There was a pair of sisters on my floor and a little girl who became my friends. They took me in so that I could listen to their records and play with them.

They were Jewish and spoke a little Yiddish, enough to make my mother comfortable. They introduced my mother to the soap operas on the radio, and that's how she learned English. And they taught my parents how to play cards so there was a social life on Friday evenings and Saturday.

But my mother had also other experiences with people who were not so kind. There was a time when my younger brother picked up a toy truck in a garbage can. He must have thrown other stuff out to get to the truck, and one woman came out of the apartment and said, "You immigrants are disgusting. We fought a war to make you safe, and this is what you teach your children to do." Unfortunately for my mother, she knew enough English at that time to understand the remark, and I can remember her crying over that.

My parents wanted so much to be American, that when I

came home from school, my mother didn't want me to speak Yiddish but only English so that she could learn from me, and my father read the *New York Times* every night. My mother learned all the American songs and studied hard for the citizenship tests.

My parents had very traditional values about moving forward through education, about being proud of being Jewish, and about maintaining certain traditions. I went to public day school, and then I went to a Hebrew school afterward to learn Hebrew and to learn about religion. My father took me to ballet school, we went to the park and to museums, and when I was a little older, he took us to Broadway, because he felt you ought to broaden your horizon and learn everything. My parents had a very active social life and made many American friends.

But in the night, I could hear my father scream. He had terrible dreams, and to this day my mother will tell you that he screams in the night as if he is being chased. There was no time when they sat me down and said, "This is what happened to us." But I do remember coming home from school and seeing my mother watch the [Adolf] Eichmann trial, and she said, "In the end he will be punished and I want to see the ending." My father could not and would not watch the trial, so they had different ways of handling it.

I know I was different from other children. My point of view was that my parents needed to be cared for. So I wrote checks for my mother and I helped her with spelling, and I wanted to protect them always from anything bad that would happen. I would never tell them anything that would give them grief or aggravation. I wanted them to he happy. I needed to take care of them so they wouldn't be hurt again.

The New York State Legislature had passed a law that gave high school diplomas to World War II veterans who had never graduated from high school. I created a graduation ceremony for those veterans, so they could get their diplomas in their own high school rather than having the diplomas just mailed to them. They came in wheelchairs and they came from nursing homes, wearing pieces of their uniforms, their medals, and their caps.

I brought my parents along that day and made a little speech. I said that my parents had been in concentration camps and that they were liberated by the Americans. American soldiers who were just boys themselves had taken off their shirts to wrap the inmates in something warm, they gave their food rations and their chocolate away, and they carried the sick out of the camps into sunlight.

These soldiers who were given diplomas that day, sixty years after the end of World War II, stood up and gave my parents a standing ovation. Among them was a veteran who was actually there when Theresienstadt was liberated, the concentration camp where my father was rescued. It was a wonderful moment for these people to come together at this age, the liberators and the people they rescued. We were *all* proud Americans.

Among my parents' proudest moments in this country were gaining American citizenship and seeing their children and grandchildren graduate from college. I am the first college graduate in my family, and my mother and father think that my being a teacher is almost as good as being president. I graduated from high school in Brooklyn and got a master's degree in guidance and counseling at Long Island University and a job teaching high school English on Staten Island. My husband pursued a Ph.D. in anthropology at New York University and became a professor at the College of Staten Island. We have two sons, Daniel and David, and they are both college graduates and recently married.

I am very proud of my parents. They raised us with a very positive attitude, loving life and looking for happiness. That's a hard thing to do when you have been through so much. I don't know if everybody understands that they, as survivors, had no older role models. When they became parents they were the oldest generation they knew and they had to leave to go to a country whose language they didn't know. As a little girl I understood that my parents had gone through a terrifying time and how lucky I was to be in a place where I never had to be as scared as they were. The people who survived the Holocaust and who came to America, their memories need to be preserved—not just *what* they went through, but *who* they were and *how* they preserved hope, especially the message that they brought with them about hope.

There were other displaced children who arrived in the United States in December 1949. Among them were ILZE JATNIEKS, age thirteen, and her brother GIRTS, age seven, who came from a displaced persons' camp in northern Germany, in the British Occupied Zone. Born in 1936, Ilze still remembers life on their farm in Latvia and their escape from the Russians in 1944.[4]

> My dad had cows, pigs, and chickens, but during the Russian occupation he was gone a lot. He would hide in the woods. In the fall of 1944 my parents and the neighbors made the decision to leave. Before we left, I think they thought they would return because they would bury things, like silverware and photo albums. We were driving our horse and buggy to Riga and then we got on a boat. We were way at the bottom, and there were a lot of people sitting on the floor. We ended up in Hamburg and then on a farm in northern Germany. While we were living there, the war ended, and then they were setting up camps around Flensburg near the Danish border.
>
> I started school in the camp with my little brother. It was just like a little Latvia there. They had church services there, we had a theater, and we had concerts. But we couldn't stay in the camps forever, so my parents found a sponsor through the Lutheran church. He was a farmer in Wisconsin. We had to go through screenings before we boarded ship. By the time we reached New York, my brother and I were sick; we came down with the measles. I can't remember coming into New York, but I remember a big area where everyone had to stand and sort out their luggage, and then we took a train to Wisconsin.
>
> My father was a farmhand there, and I went to a one-room schoolhouse. I don't remember how I learned English, but just looking at the words we learned. We started out with the little kids, and it didn't take long before we were with the older kids. Education was very important to my parents. My mother would read a lot. We always had a lot of books. I graduated from high school in Menomonie, Wisconsin. I attended Nursing School in Minneapolis and worked at Fairview Hospital before I got married. I got more involved in the Latvian community and church as I grew older.

Ilza's young brother, GIRTS JATNIEKS, born in 1942, does not remember the war and his family's flight from Latvia, but he remembers his stay in the DP camp in Flensburg.[5]

> The camp we lived in the longest (for nearly three years) was a
> soldiers' barracks, with twelve rooms, six on each side, and a
> common bathroom. One family was in each room. That was
> purely a Latvian camp until just before we moved out. Esto-
> nians moved in, and there was always friction between those
> nationalities. I remember I got into a fight with an Estonian boy.
> I was in the first and second grades in the DP camp.
>
> After four years of being here and there, our family got a
> sponsorship in Wisconsin. It was an adventure to get on the
> ship to come to America. I was kind of afraid at first because
> just before we left on the ship, I had seen a cartoon of a ship at
> sea, with a great big wave going up and the ship right on top of
> the wave, like a surfboard. I thought I was going to be like that,
> half a mile upon this big wave. I got over that! We were on the
> ship ten days, but at the end I came down with measles.
>
> I don't remember the Statue of Liberty, but I remember the
> holding area. We were there several hours with all of our crates
> and suitcases. Then we were put on the train. We came to Wis-
> consin in December 1949. There was no snow on the ground
> yet. I remember my first Christmas in the United States and my
> first Halloween the next November [sic]. My father worked long
> days as a farmhand. Then he got a job in Minneapolis working
> at a grain elevator. My mother and we children stayed behind
> in Wisconsin; my parents thought that growing up in the coun-
> try would be better for us. My father would come back from
> Minneapolis on the weekends.
>
> I finished high school in Menomonie in 1960. I wanted to
> study physics and engineering. It was cheaper for me to go to
> the University of Minnesota. Since my father had lived there
> already and paid taxes, I met the residency requirements. I joined
> the Latvian fraternity and was active with them throughout my
> college years.
>
> Right now I am the secretary for the Latvian Welfare Asso-
> ciation. We are aiding people back in Latvia, retired veterans
> with health problems and families with many children. Our local

organization gives money and support. My sister, Ilze, buys low-cost clothing and some used clothing from Goodwill. She sends boxes with clothing to orphanages and families with three or more children. Sometimes people leave legacies here in Minneapolis. We just got a few thousand dollars to help needy children in Latvia.

GUNDA GROTANS-LUSS, a sister-in-law of Ilza Jatnieks-Grotans's, arrived in the United States in June 1950. She was eight years old at the time. Born on a farm in Latvia a few months before her father died from typhus, she survived a harrowing cross-country trip to Riga, fleeing the approaching Russian troops.[6]

It was kind of last minute, and we didn't take much. Before we left we turned the animals loose that we couldn't take so they wouldn't starve, and the neighbors who stayed behind came and collected them. We were in two carts. My grandmother and my grandfather and my brother were in one cart. My mother had to walk because the second horse we had was not broken. She had to lead him and walk. As we were walking along I fell off the cart and nobody in my family noticed. Somebody who was on a bicycle and on the same road behind us picked me up.

The Germans were already retreating, and they told us not to take the main road because the Russians were bombing refugees trying to leave. It took us two weeks to get to the coast. The land route was no longer an option, so we had to leave our wagons with our barrels of flour and sugar and meat in the port. We boarded one of the ships that was going to Germany (to Danzig), one of the last ships that left in November. Some of the ships were torpedoed, so we were lucky.

We were assigned to a German farmer who was required to put up refugees. We stayed there until my birthday, which is VE [Victory in Europe] Day, May 8. I remember how food was very scarce and how the farmer slaughtered a pig, which made a lot of noise. I remember that they had a raspberry garden, and my brother and I went out and picked a few. The farmer's wife caught us and was very angry. We ran to our grandmother, and she scolded the wife in Latvian!

After that we were sent to a DP camp. In the camp, we

lived in barracks. It was in the British Occupied Zone, in northern Germany, in what is called the Lüneburger Heide [Heath].
There were lots of pine trees, meadows, and a very sandy soil-
type beach. The climate was similar to the coast of Latvia's. Initially we were locked up. There was barbed wire around the
camp, but then they relaxed the rules so we could go blueberry
picking.

I went to the first grade in the camp. My mother married a
Latvian teacher; the camp school had teachers from Latvia. A
Latvian professor who had settled in Northfield, Minnesota,
found sponsors for us who promised to give us work for a year.
Our departure was delayed because someone on our floor
caught whooping cough and we were all quarantined for two
weeks. Then they found a second sponsor for us in Blue Earth,
Minnesota.

The trip across the Atlantic was about eight days. I remember being mildly seasick. I also remember that while they were
getting ready to leave, they got rid of my teddy bear, the only
toy that was really mine, and I was rather attached to it. I was
very upset. We had to go through customs in New York. People
were stopped and searched thoroughly. Some carried antiques
in the false bottoms of their suitcases.

We went by train to Minnesota. Our sponsors were very
nice. We lived in a little house on their farm that didn't have
any central heat. It had a wood stove and an outhouse. We were
paid a hundred dollars a month, which wasn't enough for a
family of five. So my mother and grandmother contacted some
people in St. Paul, and they put us up in their house. My grandmother and mother both got jobs as cleaning ladies in an insurance company. They worked till 2:00 a.m.

I learned English in school; it took me about six months. I
was the person who interpreted for the family. We moved a lot,
so each year I was in a different school. I would just go to the
school myself and register myself. I did that the first time when
I was nine years old. I got involved with the Latvian Youth Association right away. My mother and grandmother expected that
I would attend a university. Everyone I knew planned on going
to the University of Minnesota. It was just assumed.

I went to the "U" for two years, and then I got married. My

father-in-law was fairly well-off, so he paid for me to go to the Minneapolis Institute of Art. I never felt pressured to marry a Latvian. My ex-husband, a German, was very accommodating. He was respectful of my culture. I think language is really the culture; if you don't have the language, then it is really difficult to carry on the culture. It was easy for my son to learn the language.

I took Edward to Latvia in 1989. At that point it wasn't dangerous because it was so close to independence. Given how things were before, it was a lot looser. Now the street signs are back to what they were before. They just returned them to their original names. I don't think it is always a good idea to do that. I think a certain amount of reminders is good. The Russian occupation happened for a reason, and if you remove the reminders, the reason is erased, too. I think you are more vulnerable then.

JANIS SKUJINS arrived in the United States in July 1950 at the age of ten. He was four years old when he left Latvia with his mother, who was dragging him, his one-year-old sister, and her sewing machine across the border to Germany.[7]

My father was a senior agricultural officer who became a partisan fighter when the Russians came. He stayed in the woods. They found a body that was in my father's clothing. They figured he had blown himself up to avoid being captured. I guess my mother knew then she was a widow. There was no going back.

On our way West we were moving through battle zones, and I remember bombings and cities on fire. I remember being in a basement, and I remember the door being blown open by an explosion and some shrapnel coming through the basement. My pastime, during the night, was to make sounds like people screaming. That was a prevalent sound. When the German cities were on fire you could here those strange sounds.

We moved through Germany westward. As Germany was collapsing we were looking to always be in that portion of the country where the British or the Americans were, for we knew that we were on the Russians' list for arrest or destruction. When the war finally ended, people gathered in what would eventually become DP camps.

The pleasant things in the DP camps were school and the Boy Scouts and 4-H. I remember the battles the Latvian kids and the Lithuanian kids had with slingshots. There were lots of weapons to be found, and kids had their fingers blown off by grenades. In the Boy Scout camps we would throw old live ammunition in the campfire and let it explode. I remember making zip guns when I was five or six years old and taking soldiers' beds apart. We would make swords from the quarter-inch metal rods that held the strings and have sword fights.

When we finally got into a more stable situation, my mother became the camp seamstress. All the other women would come in to have things made. I would sit under the table and listen to them gossip about who was doing what with whom. Every little kid knew that people were being raped. I remember getting a spool of insulated wire from which my mother made some bags so that she could carry some goods, and I remember stealing some carrots in a field outside a monastery. I felt very rewarded because I had stolen something good.

I had tuberculosis, so I spent a good year away from the camps, recovering in various sanitariums. Because I had TB I wasn't supposed to be allowed to go to the United States. So my mother bought an x-ray from a healthy kid. If you were younger than ten you didn't have to be x-rayed, you only needed assurance from a doctor that you were in good health. So we had an x-ray and a statement from a doctor that I was in good health, and we were able to travel together to New York.

At that time it was difficult for single widows with kids to come to the United States, but we were being sponsored by friends of my father's who had come to the United States a year earlier. We initially lived in the Bronx. My mother had met an ex-Latvian soldier in Germany, and she decided to marry him in the States. A Methodist church in Iowa sponsored him, and so, after living six months in New York, we took the train to Washington, Iowa. We arrived there in the winter. I remember the neighborhood kids peeking into the windows to see what this new kid looked like.

My stepfather was initially a carpenter, and then he got a

job as a janitor for the YMCA. My mother got a job as a janitor in the Methodist church. I was confirmed there. I had a fairly good drawing hand. There was a newspaper publisher who wanted me to draw a Christmas card for him and the Methodists wanted me to draw the church. We wanted to impress the Americans so much, my stepfather, who also had a pretty good hand, fixed my drawings so they were worth their while.

We moved to Minneapolis six years later. I remember when we came here in 1956, I could speak Latvian a lot better than the other Latvians I met because the Latvians here were speaking English to each other. When my children were born, we didn't speak English in our house. We have changed so that we speak English now as often as Latvian.

I carried the obligation of our Latvian heritage very heavily. I was raised with the knowledge that my father was a patriot and had sacrificed his life for Latvia. The only father that I acknowledged was this heroic figure. I had this sense of obligation.

The trauma of war has a way of weeding out individuals, and it is not necessarily a less-talented person who does not succeed. My mother came from a very affluent family, and she was married to an agronomist, my father, who was on track to have some considerable influence in Latvia. When she came here to the United States, all the events of the war had traumatized her to the point that she was very happy to have survived and to be a seamstress in a coat factory. She didn't have any more ambitions. She didn't earn a lot of money, but the war had taken that ambition out of her. I think the majority of the displaced persons who ended up in the United States managed to make life comfortable for themselves but really didn't pursue any greater ambitions.

10

The Paper Sons of Angel Island

Some 3,025 miles west of Ellis Island, in the San Francisco Bay, lies Angel Island. From 1910 to 1940, it was the main U.S. entry point for people who crossed the Pacific Ocean. More than a million aliens were processed at the Angel Island Immigration Station. Among the largest groups were the Chinese.

Angel Island has often been called the "Ellis Island of the West," but there were important differences between the missions of the two immigration stations. On Ellis Island, immigrants from Europe were generally welcomed to the United States, and the vast majority were processed and landed immediately. Over a span of more than sixty years less than 5 percent of the newcomers were excluded from the United States.[1] By contrast, on Angel Island, many Asian immigrants were allowed entry only grudgingly. Eventually, some 80 to 90 percent of the arrivals were admitted after they had been detained and interrogated. The average length of detention was about two weeks, but the Chinese faced great variations in the lengths of their detentions.[2]

In the mid- and late nineteenth century, when there were no restrictive immigration laws, large numbers of Chinese had come to the United States, first drawn by the Gold Rush in California and then by the opportunity to work—for low wages—on the first transcontinental railroad. An economic depression in the United States in the 1870s, however, fueled strong anti-Chinese sentiments. In response to public opinion, the U.S. Congress passed the Chinese Exclusion Laws—the first was passed in May 1882—to restrict the entry of Chinese immigrants.[3]

* The first exclusion law barred the immigration of Chinese laborers for ten years. The act did grant exemptions to certain groups of people: travelers, teachers, students, merchants, and relatives of American-born Chinese or of Chinese who had been naturalized prior to the passage of the law and who had left families behind in China.

* A major event affecting Chinese immigration was the fire that struck San Francisco after the 1906 earthquake. It destroyed most birth and citizenship records kept in the city and led many Chinese to claim that they had been born in the United States, that their birth records had been destroyed, and that they were American citizens. American citizenship would allow them to travel back to China, to claim children born in China (where there were no official birth records because Chinese women usually delivered at home), and to bring them to the United States.

The immigration service at Angel Island thus had to rely on applicants' and witnesses' testimony to verify their birthplace and membership in an "exempt status." This job was time consuming, for an estimated 175,000 Chinese immigrants were processed and detained in the station's barracks from 1910 to 1940. Most of these newcomers had taken the "crooked path" to immigration. In attempting to immigrate to the United States, these "paper sons" and "paper daughters" used false papers that claimed they were children of American citizens or exempt residents.

For a fee, individuals provided "paper children" and their "paper parents" with information that offered evidence of a familial relationship, false testimonies on the individual's behalf, and false identification papers with fake photographs attached. The "paper sons" industry became a thriving business, and people also wrote "coaching books" to prepare them for the immigration inspectors' interrogations.[4] Coaching books were usually given to would-be immigrants before they departed China for the United States so that they could study them on the sea voyage to San Francisco, memorize their contents, and then throw them overboard to evade detection. The number and nature of questions asked in the Angel Island interrogations were such that coaching papers were deemed a necessity by *both* legal and illegal Chinese immigrants and their U.S.-based sponsors.

The immigration officers asked the newcomers in meticulous detail about their family, their house, and their neighborhood and then compared their answers with those of other witnesses who were able to testify on their behalf. If the answers given by all parties were similar, the new arrival would be landed; if not he would receive deportation orders that could be appealed. If the applicant wished to appeal, the copy of his testimony would be sent to the central office in Washington, D.C. The majority of the appeals were granted on the basis of these transcripts.

According to the testimony of an immigration inspector, most of the Chinese newcomers were pretty young. "There were many boys coming through—twelve, fourteen, fifteen years old—a lot of them smart kids. They were very sure of themselves. . . . I think it was remarkable that the applicants were rather stoical. They stood up well, by and large."[5]

It took a world war before President Franklin Roosevelt repealed the Chinese exclusion laws on December 17, 1943. Citing the need "to correct a historic mistake," Chinese immigration was placed under the same quota system that regulated European immigration. By then, many Chinese "paper sons" were serving in the armed forces or working in defense-related industries. Here are the stories of five immigrants who "stood up well."

* * *

BENJAMIN CHOY was thirteen years old in 1930 when he arrived at Angel Island with a "paper brother." Both boys were the "paper sons" of a Chinese family in San Francisco that had two American-born children.[6]

> I had a cousin take me from my village in southern China to Hong Kong. We stayed in a hostel by the waterfront for one night. The next day he sent me off to America on the steamship *President McKinley*. My paper brother and I stayed in steerage in the rear part of the ship, where they had a whole bunch of bunks and a whole bunch of people. It was a pretty

long voyage from China to San Francisco, some twenty-one days, and I was seasick most of the time. When I would go up on the deck, I could see seagulls following the ship and miles and miles of ocean.

We arrived in San Francisco early in the morning. When I looked at the city and saw the big buildings and the bright lights twinkling I was amazed. I thought we would land there, but instead they took us to Angel Island for temporary confinement and interrogation, to make sure that everything was OK, before they permitted us to go ashore. So I stayed there with my paper brother in a barracks-like building, full of two-tiered bunk beds, with a big crowd of new arrivals who were all men.

For dining, we sat at a big table split into several sections. They had a lot of rice and some Chinese food, maybe three or four dishes for lunch or dinner. A bathroom on Angel Island was like a lineup of showers. For sleeping, my paper brother got the upper bunk and I got the lower bunk. We stayed there for about two weeks. And when it came to interrogation, they called me first.

Before we embarked, at the beginning of the trip, they had sent me a booklet; it was filled with questions and answers. You were supposed to learn the answers from these booklets. So when they would ask, "Who is your father? Who is your mother? And how old are you" you would know. "You got a brother?" and you would say, "Yes." And they'd ask, "What's his name?" They called that booklet "the paper." It takes a long time to memorize all that. You have to be coached, but they didn't ask me anything from what I was coached! They just asked where I lived, how many rooms there were in my house, where it was located. So I just kept recounting what I knew of my own house.

What I told the examiner my paper brother would not know, because he came from a different family. So during lunch break, very quickly, I went to inform my paper brother about the facts I told the examiner. He said exactly what I said. I think that's why the examiner believed we were brothers. I don't know how the examiner could tell we were related, because we came with different photographs. My photograph was from a different place, and my paper brother's came from a different photographer. I mean, it was ridiculous, but we got away with it!

It is pretty tough, coming as a paper son. Actually it is illegal. But when you are a kid you are not intending to lie; you just follow what the grown-ups tell you to do. My "paper parents" actually had a son and a daughter, not two sons. The reason they reported a second son is that they could sell the paper twice to make more money.

I was in the fifth grade when I left China. I learned the English alphabet from our neighbor in the village. When I came here I didn't have the opportunity to continue my Chinese, because I had to learn a new language. I tried hard to pronounce English so that people could understand me. It took me a long time to practice in front of a mirror to get it right.

During World War II, I was working in the shipyards, building victory ships for the Department of Defense. I was an assistant to the chief electrical engineer. I took a correspondence course from the National Radio Institute. I studied radio and television and electronics, so I would have an electrical background. It took me two years, and I got a diploma for that. When World War II broke out, I got the job in the shipyards because I had that electronics knowledge. Since I had all that knowledge, I got a deferment to stay with the shipyards, building ships. I was naturalized in the 1950s, and then I worked for the Bechtel Company in its engineering office.

It's good for people in this country, besides the Chinese, to go over to Angel Island, to look, and then to rethink the past. They are already doing that. They are making things much easier now for those who want to come here to be part of this country, to make something of themselves. Some Chinese kids come over here, and they have a chance to go to college, to the university, and then they have the knowledge to make some kind of contribution. They have already contributed a lot of things! In the old days people were prejudiced, especially during times when the economy was bad. When the Chinese came over here, they had to build this country up, building the railroads—really hard labor. Although the Chinese took the low-paying jobs, still the people here said, "Gee, we don't want these people here because they are taking our jobs." That's why they passed Exclusion Laws.

Of course, now they don't have those laws anymore. People are better educated and more worldly. But this country still has a problem with racism. We've got black and white and others—all kinds of different people—so bias, prejudice, is bound to exist. But we are trying to associate with each other and get along as well as possible.

JAMES LOUIE was eleven years old when he arrived at Angel Island in 1932. His grandfather had arranged his passage to come to the United States for a better future.[7]

My paper father was my uncle, who was already in America. He himself came to this country as a paper son. He fabricated a village and all the family names in the village. A good number of them were paper sons. I remember a schoolteacher who would coach me.

When I got off the *President Coolidge* after a twenty-one-day voyage from Hong Kong to San Francisco, we got on a little tug. I wasn't especially scared, but I was curious. When the tug arrived at the pier on Angel Island, all of us had to leave our suitcases in a warehouse right at the dock. We just took a few essential things to the barracks where we stayed. Once a week, we were allowed to go down to the pier and get whatever we wanted from our luggage.

The Chinese always complained about the conditions on Angel Island. You could see that by all the poems written on the wall. Actually I didn't think that it was that bad, but I was just a kid. There were three meals a day. The food was simple, but it was much better than what we had back in the village.

There was a gentleman who got detained at Angel Island for months and months, and he knew English. And he taught English to whoever wanted to get in a class. So I had English classes. We got to play outside, and we would catch pigeons, there were so many of them. We got hot water to pluck the feathers, and we would take them to the cooks, who would cook them for us.

I was questioned three different times. The examiners asked all kinds of questions about your village, your grandmother, and how many windows do you have in your house? They also always questioned the paper father (my uncle) and my paper brother (my cousin) as witnesses. Whatever was not written down beforehand, whatever was not prearranged, then the answers you gave wouldn't be the same among all three of you. We didn't match up.

They were going to deport me. My paper father (who had been in the United States before) appealed to the court. It cost him a hundred dollars; he had to bribe the immigration officials through a Chinese go-between. Finally, I was admitted "as a native, parole evidence."

After James left Angel Island he took the train to Pittsburgh, where his grandfather lived. After going to school in Pittsburgh and serving in the armed forces, he worked for Standard Oil in China.

I think the most important thing is that we look at other people as human beings. They should be equal. Back in high school, there was a group of kids who became my lifelong friends. They treated me very much as an equal. They didn't look down on me, and they never despised me. We were friends. Some of them are still my friends. I guess I just happened to be in a town that was that way. Not all the towns were.

ALBERT KAI WONG arrived at Angel Island as a twelve-year-old in 1934. He came to join his father in the United States and to get a better education. His story became the subject of a children's book, *Kai's Journey to Gold Mountain*.[8] Sixty-six years after his arrival, he remembered:

I came from Hong Kong on the American President Line aboard the *Hoover*. My mother and brother were crying when I left. The trip took twenty-one days. We went to Angel Island by ferry. It was like wild country. I remember the wooden plank walk to the left and up the hill to a big building, the Administration Building. We were separated into small groups, stripped, and given a physical examination.

Then we were assigned to one big barrack exclusively Chinese. There were rows and rows of bunk beds. Mine was at the

end of the building going out to a volleyball court. When the
grown-ups were not playing basketball, we kids would play
our games. Early in the morning we would line up for breakfast and do the same thing for lunch and suppertime. My father
knew some of the people who worked in the kitchen, and I
would always get extra stuff that my father sent over.

I was interrogated several times. People around me were
worried all the time. They had come in fictitiously, and they
had to learn what answers were correct. They asked about your
family, your house, etc. So I told them what I knew. They asked
a lot of stupid questions. I remember at my house in the village
we had an orchard. The interrogator asked me, "How many
steps are there going down?" And I didn't know, I didn't count
them. And they said, "You mean you went up and down there
every day and you don't remember?" I said, "You go up and
down the stairs here every day. You tell me how many steps
there are." And they cracked up, laughing.

For me it was relatively easy because I was legitimate. My
grandfather lived in San Francisco on Vallejo Street, and my
father was in business in San Jose. So I stayed only a short time
[at Angel Island]. I wasn't scared. I had playmates, and the
people in the kitchen would bring letters to me from my father.
I didn't see him until five weeks had passed, and they let me
out. Then my father came to pick me up. Three years later my
mother and my two younger brothers came. I grew up in San
Jose.

At the time, I didn't feel bad about the experience I had on
Angel Island, but now that I look back, it was uncalled for. Why
should we be locked behind bars? They looked down at you—
the interrogators, the guards. I didn't know about the Chinese
Exclusion Law until I went to school. When I found out about
the law, I was hurt. I was in the air force for five years, and I
know we would treat prisoners of war that way. But these were
immigrants, looking for better education and better living conditions. That's mainly why everyone came to America—for the
opportunity.

JOHN LUI arrived at Angel Island in 1936 at the age of twelve. He
was sponsored by an uncle whose father had come to California to

work on the railroad. Both his uncle and his grandfather were American citizens.[9]

> My father died very young. My brother, second to me, passed away soon after my father, and then my sister did. So three people in my family died. We could not find a doctor—or anyone—to help them. So I decided I should become a doctor. To become a doctor I had to get out of China, because there were no opportunities in China to do anything. My family had no money.
>
> I came with a different family. I was supposed to be one of their sons. We were separated on the trip because of my age, twelve. They consider that independent, that you can live by yourself. The rest of them lived in a different class on the boat coming over; it was the *President Lincoln*. I was living with hundreds of people, young and old, in the freight hole. The beds were stacked up two high.
>
> The trip took a little over two weeks. I got sick many times once we started sailing. I used to go up on the deck and try to lean over and throw up, and the water would come splashing through and I got wet. In some ways I was feeling bad that I was leaving my family in China and all my friends there. In another way I really looked forward to the trip.
>
> Those who left for America went back to China to get married. Every time they went back, they would declare that they had a child. They built a whole family tree like that, and they would say, "We have one opening. One of our children died, and if you want to become one of us, we will take you." That was my golden opportunity.
>
> In order to come here you'd better know the whole family history and everything about your village and surroundings — everything—when you go through immigration. Each of us got a little booklet written in Chinese, telling us all the potential questions they might ask us so every member of the family would be identical in their answers or at least they would match. I remember quite a bit of the questioning: "Who lives next door to you?" There is somebody to the right, there is somebody to the left, and they asked the name, the age of the children, and how many houses there were in your village. "And what does

your house look like?" They wanted to screen out the guy who really didn't belong to the family. So we were briefed on that beforehand. And then the booklet with all that information was thrown into the Pacific Ocean.

When the boat landed in San Francisco, there was a smaller boat that met us. They would usher the immigrants to the smaller boat and sail for Angel Island. We just walked in columns from the deck to the detention barracks. Our luggage was stowed away in a warehouse. The first thing we saw was a big barracks that housed about two hundred people. You were packed like sardines in there and just stayed and waited until you were called for interrogation. There was a basketball court in the back of the barracks. So a lot of people played basketball to pass the time away. I was there for two weeks before they called me for an interview.

Personally I was never scared. When you go through Angel Island you have only one thing in mind, to get through that detention period and to be able to land in the United States and pursue the ambitions you have. But I was feeling bad for the people who didn't make it, who wrote the sad poetry on the wall.

It was such a happy moment in my life when my uncle came and said, "Well, we are going to leave for San Francisco." My uncle brought in a friend with a car who met us at the pier and drove us to Chinatown. So that was the first time I had a chance to ride in a car. And then there was the first time I saw a telephone. We had no telephone in China, no electricity, and the only light we had was candlelight.

The first thing I did was to join the Chinese Baptist church. That church helped me pick up English, gave me a chance to meet native-born people, and listen to both English and Chinese sermons on Sunday. The English class was taught by a missionary who also played the piano and taught Sunday school. I sang in the choir. I learned English pretty fast. In six months, I was already in junior high school in San Francisco, and the missionary lady asked me to interpret for her on Sundays.

I first lived with my paper family in Chinatown and went to school from there. Within six months I was lucky to be introduced to an American family who took me in and treated me like a son. I cleaned house and cooked for them and washed dishes. They gave me the key to the house, so I could do anything I liked. I wanted some pocket money and to save some money, so I became a shoe shine boy on weekends.

I worked in the parks of San Francisco, carrying shoe shine boxes and saying, "Shine, mister? Shine, mister? Ten cents a shoe!" It would take me half an hour to polish a pair of shoes. I also sold newspapers. I graduated from junior high school within two years, went to high school for two and a half years, and then joined the U.S. Army (Air Force) a few months after Pearl Harbor. Soaking wet, I weighed ninety-five pounds.

I was a very top-notch aircraft mechanic. I knew the B-17, B-25, the fighter planes. I could fix anything. Eventually they sent me to study to become a mechanic for the B-29, the plane that dropped the atomic bomb. They wanted to send me overseas with the crew. But they decided maybe I would be more valuable to stay in the United States and be kept alive.

I am not angry about having to go through Angel Island. I never considered it a prison or detention camp. We were told that we would have to go through certain procedures. Today, when you go to the University of California to study, you have to take a test. Simple as that. I accepted it. We never were mistreated, and they didn't beat you up. We were well fed and cared for, except it was so crowded. It was the people who got sent back that felt bad. I think you and I can see that.

I considered Angel Island a gate to opportunity. You have to go through a certain test, a step at a time. That's the way I feel. The people who didn't have the education I had, or the desire or the capability to attain something, they stayed in Chinatown, earning low salaries. They are the ones who noticed a big difference in the reaction of the American people toward them. But for me, I had only one ambition: I wanted to become a doctor or an engineer. I was aiming for that. If I had stayed in China, I'd be a nobody today. In the United States, I was the first one in my family, the only one from my village, to graduate from college. I have accomplished a lot of stuff in my lifetime.

In 1940 ten-year-old HOP JEONG came to Angel Island as the "son of a son of a citizen." His grandfather, who lived in San Francisco but visited China periodically, had created a family of nine "paper children." Hop Jeong became the son of one of these children.[10]

I knew nothing about America. All I learned from my grandfather, who'd come back from San Francisco, was that this was the land of opportunity, of gold, and of free education. I came alone on the *President Coolidge* from Hong Kong and arrived at Angel Island in September 1940. I remember keeping my coaching notes until the time came to destroy them. I remember questions about the town I was growing up in, the layout of our house, who slept in each room. These were easier to answer than questions about our phony "paper" family.

I don't remember anything extraordinary happening while I was staying at Angel Island. For all I knew it was like going to a camp. We were all waiting for our turn to get processed and enter this country. One of the questions I missed was just foolish to ask a ten-year-old child: to prove that I was in this "paper" relationship with my father and eight uncles, I had to know the names of all these uncles and their birthdays.

In Chinatown in those days, most of the people I ran around with were immigrants, and so we all knew we were all "phonies," to say the least. I just thought that was the way of life. Living in Chinatown, then, was like living in a ghetto. When we first arrived we stayed in a rooming house. My grandfather was sharing this ten-by-ten-foot room with another man and myself and my younger brother, my "paper" cousin. After six months, we moved to another building where we had a ten-by-ten-foot room for ourselves, just the three of us. We were there for a number of years, until we had first crack at living in a housing project for low-income families. So we moved into this two-bedroom, one-bath, kitchen apartment, amazed to have all that space.

I served for two years in a military intelligence unit, with one year as a clerk typist in Korea, interrogating South Korean POWs who were returning from North Korea. Being in the army during the Korean War was helpful in becoming a naturalized citizen, and so was the amnesty program (by the INS) that helped us get our records straight about our true family relationships. Then, I mentioned that I had another "true" brother in Hong Kong, and he became eligible (under the new 1965 immigration law) to come to the United States. I sponsored him in 1997 to come to this country because he was concerned about the Chinese takeover of Hong Kong. So of the whole family, he is the only one who came here *legitimately*.

I went to San Francisco State and then to Golden Gate College, where I got my master of business administration (MBA). After college I got a job in the accounting department at Kaiser Hospital, where I worked for thirty-three years. I spent the last ten years of my working life preparing income taxes part-time. Now I am doing it full time.

When I went back to Angel Island with my three girls and two grandchildren, my eight-year-old granddaughter saw a movie there that showed armed guards, and she thought I had been in jail. Yet going back to it physically didn't bring back brutal, bad memories for me. But future generations should know about Angel Island and the Chinese Exclusion Act. Even myself, until twenty-five years ago, was not aware of this act. It is the only law that excluded an ethnic group, and not many people are aware of that. I think it is something that people *should* be aware of. You might say the Jewish people have their Holocaust and the Japanese have their detention camps and this is all part of history. But very few people are aware of Angel Island and what it represents.

In the night from August 11 to 12, 1940, a fire broke out in the Administration Building of Angel Island. Eleven-year-old Myron Wong, son of a Chinese father, born in the United States, was among the detainees who escaped unharmed. He remembers, "My brother and I got some clothes on and some blankets and ran out. That night they had to put us up in a horse stable. Everybody was pretty calm. Nobody was panicking."[11]

No one was injured, and it was determined that the fire was not set deliberately. but the station's detainees and officials were moved to San Francisco. After making improvements to the structures, the station was used again in World War II to house enemy aliens. Among them was the merchant marine crew of a German ship, the

SS *Columbus*, which her captain had scuttled off the coast near Cape May.

The area that had been the quarantine station was turned over to the state of California in 1954. Some of the poetry the Chinese detainees wrote on the building's walls is still visible. Today Angel Island is a National Historic Landmark and a California State Park.

* * *

What makes Angel Island unique is that it represents the best and worst in American attitudes toward immigration. Erika Lee, granddaughter of Chinese immigrants, summarizes those attitudes succinctly in the epilogue of her book *At America's Gates*: "We are indeed a nation of immigrants, but we are also a gate keeping nation, and it is the tension between these two identities that continues to shape not only America's ambivalent immigration policy, but also Americans' ambivalence about immigrants."[12]

11

Risk and Protective Factors in the Lives of Immigrant Children

The fifty voices that tell their stories in this book belong to immigrants from Europe, the Middle East, and China who came to the United States as children during the first half of the twentieth century. At that time some 10 to 15 percent of the U.S. population was foreign born. That immigrant influx is rivaled today by a wave of newcomers from Latin America, Asia, and Africa. At the beginning of the twenty-first century, 20 percent of the children in the United States are the offspring of immigrants.

Surprisingly little is known about immigrant children's psychological experiences and their impact on the children's development and well-being.[1] The oral histories of the child immigrants who came through Ellis and Angel islands show us, in retrospect, that the process of "becoming an American" is slow and complex. Most came to the United States in middle childhood; the average age of the girls was ten and that of the boys, twelve. It took these small strangers many decades of living until they felt that they truly belonged here.

When they shared their stories with the interviewers from Ellis and Angel islands, the "child immigrants" were in their sixties and seventies. They had reached an age when they were engaged in

139

what the gerontologist Robert Butler has called "a life review," with "memory serving a sense of self and its continuity."[2] Dramatic and emotional situations, such as those surrounding the process of immigrating and adapting to a new country, tend to produce fixed and lasting memories, hence the poignancy and emotional power of their narratives.[3]

Wherever possible, I have sought out additional sources of information to substantiate statements of fact made in individual oral histories. They include written documents that deal with the historical events that "framed" the individuals' lives: World War I, the Great Depression, the rise and fall of Hitler's rule, World War II, and the displacement of millions after World War II ended. The oral histories of family members who immigrated with a particular child (sisters, brothers, and future spouses and their siblings) or who settled in the same communities in the United States also served as a check of the individual narratives' reliability and validity.

Across all ethnic lines, the child immigrants' life stories tell a remarkable tale of *human resilience,* or their ability to overcome great odds in the face of nearly insurmountable obstacles. Much has been made of immigration's hardships and the negative impact of the immigration experience on family life. The oral histories of the children of Ellis and Angel islands offer us the opportunity to balance this view by looking at the protective factors that made a positive impact on their development despite the presence of numerous risk factors and stressful life events.

Risk Factors and Stressful Life Events

The narratives of the child immigrants are filled with accounts of common hardships experienced *before* and *after* their parents' decision to emigrate. They recounted the grinding poverty of the tenant farmers in China, Italy, and Scandinavia; the financial hardships of urban middle-class families in Germany and Great Britain during the Depression that followed World War I; the political persecution and extermination of the Armenians in Turkey and of the Jews in Russia, Poland, Germany, and Austria; the loss of loved ones who died in World War I and World War II; and the loss of one's homeland among the displaced persons of Eastern Europe.

The immigration experience itself could be equally stressful. Confronted with a new language and new customs, child immigrants soon learned that the streets of their new land were not paved with gold. Most lived under precarious economic conditions and in crowded neighborhoods. Some, especially the Chinese, the Irish, the Italians, and the Jews, would encounter prejudice in school and at work.

Immigrant parents often relied on their children's labor to "make do." Whether it involved caring for siblings, shopping, cooking, scavenging in the streets, selling newspapers, shining shoes, or doing other work inside or outside the home, income pooling became necessary because of the low wages the newcomers earned. Immigrant children not only became wage earners but also interpreters and guides for their parents in their dealing with landlords, local bureaucrats, school officials, and shopkeepers.

Yet despite many stressful events in their lives, few child immigrants reported lasting emotional trauma that impeded their adaptation to life in a new country. There were some exceptions, notably among the Jewish children who escaped from Hitler's Third Reich. One female, who came alone on a Kindertransport, suffered for years from survivors' guilt. She turned to alcohol as a solace, as did her oldest daughter, and continued to drink after her first husband's death. She considers herself now a "recovering alcoholic."

A Jewish male, born in Vienna, recounted his father's nervous breakdown once his family had reached America and the chronic depression that left him unable to keep a job. Another Jewish boy, born in Berlin, was plagued by repeated attacks of a "nervous stomach" ailment once he made it safely to the United States. He considers himself fortunate, "because I came through with a degree of normalcy." By contrast, his younger brother developed serious emotional problems, was placed in a separate foster home a year and a half after their arrival, and never managed to develop any stable social relationships in adulthood.

These are the exceptions. The majority of the child immigrants, according to their own accounts, put down roots and managed to make a decent life for themselves in their new country. They mastered the English language, graduated from high school or even college, found a job and a permanent place to live, married, bought a home, and launched their children toward a better life. Moreover, they became citizens who appreciated their constitutional rights—the foremost being equal protection and justice under the law and the freedom of expression—which native-born Americans take for granted. The immigrants knew how precious these rights are.

Protective Factors

Most child immigrants considered the *support their family members provided* as a major protective factor in their adaptation to a new life in a new country. That support included the advice and assistance of members of the extended family who had immigrated to the United States at an earlier time. Uncles, aunts, cousins, older siblings, and fathers had often emigrated years before the rest of their family left their countries, and they had saved money so they might pay for their family's passage and find cheap housing for them.

Fathers were often strangers to the child immigrants, especially to the Jewish children from Russia or Poland. Many had only seen fading photos of their fathers dressed in orthodox garb and with a long beard. Then they met clean-shaven fathers at the entry to Ellis Island. Upon seeing her father for the first time at age four, Kate Simon remembered, he "looked like a God to me. He, whose existence I had doubted, was absolutely gorgeous."

DONALD ROBERTS, a twelve-year-old Welsh boy, was old enough to appreciate the labor and backbreaking work his father did during the Great Depression:

> He would dig drainage ditches and get about thirty dollars a month. He'd take a couple of potatoes with him and make a fire, and that's what he ate. When things started to ease up a bit, he would go up and down the streets [in New York], looking for some construction going on, trying to get a little job— one street after the other, day after day. I thank him so much for having the courage to give us the opportunity to live here in this country.

Uncles and aunts also helped build a bridge for the immigrant children between the old country and the new. They became sponsors who found temporary housing and jobs for these children's parents and their older siblings and could be counted on for an emergency loan. Their offspring, the "American cousins," would introduce the young newcomers to their neighborhood's street language and to the wondrous customs of chewing gum, peeling bananas and oranges, and eating hot dogs and peanut butter sandwiches. Chewing gum, especially, was mystifying to many child immigrants.

Remembered the seventeen-year-old Irish lass Johanna Flaherty when she met her aunt at Ellis Island:

> We got on the El [train], and . . . I couldn't imagine how come everybody on the train was chewing and nobody was putting food in their mouths. A few days later I learned it was chewing gum. I had a lot of cousins who took me everywhere to see different things. I really enjoyed the first day we went to Coney Island. I had a hot dog and wondered, O my gosh, what's this? I would call it a sausage, but they kept calling them hot dogs.

And twelve-year-old Edward Rune Myrbeck was introduced by a Swedish uncle, who lived in the Midwest, to the mystery of a gum machine. "That's candy," he said, and dropped a penny in there, gave the gumball to me, and being a polite kid, I put it in my mouth and started chewing . . . and tried to talk at the same time. I walked at least a mile and half . . . before I swallowed it. My uncle said, "Oh, you shouldn't do that." But in Sweden you could never spit . . . when you were walking down the street.

Uncles and aunts cared for half orphans who had lost their fathers in World War I. They took under their wing girls such as ten-year-old Inge Nastke, who went with her grandparents from Hamburg to her aunt's ranch in Montana, and fifteen-year-old Dora Essel, who traveled with two cousins from eastern Germany to work in her aunt's bakery in Baltimore. She remembered, "My cousins who spoke only English with me used to call me 'Dumb Dora.' . . . But [my aunt] was like a second mother to me, and she taught me many things."

These relatives also saved the lives of children orphaned during the Armenian massacre and Jewish children who escaped persecution during Hitler's reign in Germany and Austria. "My aunt was a wonderful woman," said John Alabilikian. "She saved me and fourteen young girls who were taken away from their parents."

By far the *most important source of support* for most child immigrants was their *mothers,* many of whom made significant economic contributions to the household both *before* and *after* immigration.

Their children, especially their daughters, highly valued their mothers' competence and encouragement.

Kate Simon's observations could apply to many of these extraordinary women: "My mother went back to work when we entered school [after my father deserted us]. She was a very independent person with an extraordinary intelligence that never had the opportunity to develop. She had visions of my going to school." Kate, herself, would become a well-known travel writer.

The immigrant mothers tended to have more basic skills that transferred from the "old" country to the new one, and they adapted more quickly than the fathers did. Ample evidence shows that assets and earned income under the mothers' control were more often spent on items relating to their children's health and well-being than similar resources under the fathers' control.

Mothers took cleaning jobs in other people's homes, in offices, in schools, and in public buildings; they worked as housekeepers and cooks; they toiled in restaurants and bakeries; or they labored in garment factories. They became janitors in schools and churches and took in boarders. One mother became a superintendent in a New York apartment building. "[I]t meant that our family would have a much-needed second income without my mother having to leave us alone at home," said her oldest son, who became a radio astronomer.

Other mothers would continue to work as seamstresses, work they had begun in Europe to support their families. A sewing machine was one of the most treasured assets they brought across the Atlantic, sometimes under considerable hardship. Asta Andersen Hoglind, who came to the United States as a seven-year-old, remembers her mother's distress when she saw her sewing machine standing on the pier all by itself when their ship was about to leave the harbor in Copenhagen. "She was all upset because that was the one thing she had used a lot and would need in the United States. So she immediately went to the captain, and he saw to it that it was brought on board ship. She had that machine for years . . . because she always sewed."

JANIS SKUJNINS from Latvia remembers that his mother dragged him (a four-year-old at the time), his one-year-old sister, and her sewing machine across the border to Germany while fleeing the Russian invasion.

> Where did she get the tenacity to do that? She was on foot, and
> her friends would come by on a horse and wagon, and they
> would tell her there wasn't any room to put us up there. . . .
> When she came here to the United States, all the events of the
> war had traumatized her to the point that she was very happy
> to have survived and to be a seamstress in a coat factory.

The most important skill the child immigrants needed to acquire was *fluency in speaking and reading English*. They did so at an impressive speed. It did not seem to matter whether their native language was Armenian, Cantonese, German, Italian, Russian, Polish, Danish, Swedish, Finish, Latvian, or Yiddish. They were usually able to speak English within a year after their arrival in the United States.

In school the immigrant children confronted the new language most intensely. They also learned English by attending special classes that churches and public libraries offered and by watching movies that played in neighborhood cinemas. As they struggled with the new language, their native-born classmates gave them nicknames like "Dago," "Greenhorn," "Heinie," "Popcorn," "Square Head," and "Wop." It took enormous determination and discipline for a child to manage a new language under these circumstances.

Many child immigrants considered *a caring teacher* as one of the most important positive influences in their young lives. Said Sally Kleinman Gurian, who had come from the Ukraine at age eight, "We didn't know any English, and in school we sat in a large class with a lot of immigrant children. . . . So we studied real hard. We managed to get through very well, and we loved school. We had very good teachers and they were very patient with us." Rose Levine, who came from Russia at age eleven, had a teacher who knew how to speak Yiddish. "Miss Creitel . . . was very nice. She spoke to me in Jewish and explained to me what she was teaching. I was very anxious to learn, and I felt good because I was learning English. So I learned fast and got good marks."

Oreste Teglia, who was twelve when he immigrated, was placed in a Catholic parochial school in Chicago. "The teacher found out that I was good with clay. So she asked me to make animals, and put them on the windowsill, and I eventually learned a few English words. The last school I attended was run by nuns. . . they would give me elocution lessons once a week, which helped a lot."

After he arrived in the United States from Armenia, eight-year-old Vozchan Parsegian was put in a special class in school. He recalls, "I guess we were pretty much all immigrants. The teachers were kind and did remarkably well with us. By the time I got to the seventh grade the teacher made me her favorite, as she would tell my mother when she would come to visit the school."

INGE NASTKE remembered,

> I went to school and the other children thought I was an oddball. I tried very hard to speak English. In one year I was able to speak it without any mistakes. . . . I had lovely teachers who were patient with me. After school, one of them said to me, "Inge, you and I will have a little talk," and she explained many things that were new to me. She was very kind and understanding.

Another German girl, EMMI KREMER, age nine, arrived in Brooklyn and started school the very next day. She said,

> The first weeks in school were rough. The students would tease me and call me "Heinie." Nobody wanted to be associated with that word. So the teacher asked the class, "Does anybody speak German?" And one girl raised her hand, and it was through her that I learned my first words of English. . . . Within a year's time I learned how to speak English—the American way.

Once the child immigrants became fluent in English, they learned to appreciate the treasures they could find in the public library. Kate Simon remembered in her Bronx neighborhood "the best place of all . . . was the library. It was a great adventure. We could take out two books, and the librarians were terribly nice. The idea that there were all these books, and . . . I had the privilege of reading them, was very exciting."

And Irving Halperin recalled, "I was an omnivorous reader. I read all the time, every book in the public library [in Bayonne, New Jersey]. I used to enjoy reading historical novels. I knew so much history, I used to drive the teachers crazy in school. I had one teacher who wanted to get rid of me, so she skipped me a grade."

Emmi Kremer reminisced, "But not far from where we lived

there was a library. And I lived in that library. I was always reading. And I always wanted to write."

Young immigrant children were as likely as their native-born peers to be enrolled in elementary school, but their ranks thinned out in high school. Even fewer attended college, but there were exceptions. Among children of Armenian, Chinese, German, and Jewish backgrounds who came from middle-class families, nearly a third of the boys and one-fifth of the girls went on to college and entered a profession. The college-educated boys became accountants, astronomers, lawyers, engineers, physicists, and priests. Among the college-educated girls were artists, authors, counselors, nurses, teachers, and the founder of a progressive experimental school.

Participating in their churches' social activities created supportive links for teenage immigrants between the old world and the new. It didn't matter what religious affiliation their parents had, the young people enjoyed the company of others of the same faith. Harry Singer and his family came from the Ukraine, and he enjoyed a social life that "centered around people who attended the same synagogue." He even met his future wife at a dance sponsored at the Young Men's Hebrew Association.

Asta Andersen Hoglind joined a Danish folk dance group that a Lutheran church in Brooklyn sponsored. "We had a lot of good times," she remembered. "We had Christmas tree parties where the big tree was put up, and we danced around it in the traditional style. . . . I married Knute in that church. That was our life—the church. Not that we were religious fanatics, but it was a place to meet nice people, contemporaries."

Clara Honold, who had come from Germany, joined a Lutheran church in St. Albans, New York. Like the Danish immigrants, she especially enjoyed the celebrations on Christmas Eve, which reminded her of the customs of her childhood. The displaced children from the Baltic countries also found a "little Latvia" in the church services they attended in Minneapolis and felt at home there.

John Lui, who came from China to San Francisco at age twelve, joined the Chinese Baptist church in San Francisco. "That church helped me pick up English, gave me a chance to meet native-born people. . . . I sang in the choir. I learned English pretty fast. In six months . . . the missionary lady [who played the piano and taught Sunday School] asked me to interpret for her on Sundays."

As they became teenagers, the young immigrants took a great deal of responsibility for their families' well-being. Psychologists would say they practiced "required helpfulness." The oral histories of the children who came from Ellis and Angel islands are filled with vivid descriptions of the strategies they used to balance the demands of school with the necessity of work.

In some cases, immigrant girls had an easier time finding jobs than immigrant boys did. There was a steady demand for domestic help, and Dora Essel, Emmi Kremer, and Annette Terlizzi Monouydas, among other girls, worked in the family business, bakeries, restaurants, and grocery stores. Annette remembers, "All we had to do, it seems, was just work, go to school and work, go to school and work. That's all we used to do. And the business was seven days a week." During Prohibition she had to hide bootlegged whiskey in the woods, digging holes and covering the bottles up, and when people came, she had to go and dig them out again in rain, shine, or snow.

Celia Adler, who came alone to the United States as a twelve-year-old to join her sisters, got a job as a dressmaker—at four dollars a week—and learned English in night school. Until he graduated Harry Singer worked in a leather factory from 6:00 to 8:00 a.m. and then went to high school. And EDWARD CORSI, who immigrated from Italy at age ten and would eventually become the Commissioner of Immigration and Naturalization at Ellis Island, remembered:

> When I was old enough for my first job, I went to work as a lamplighter, rising at four in the morning to put out the lamps on my route. Then I would have breakfast and get to school by nine. Contributing what little I could to the limited family income, I was in turn a lamplighter, messenger, and clerk in a telegraph office.

When he first arrived as a twelve-year-old in Chicago, Oreste Teglia did all the chores—the cooking, baking, washing, and babysitting—at home while his parents and older sister went to work. When he was fifteen years old, he left school and got a work permit. "I sold newspapers, I worked in a nut factory, and I made banana bushels at the market—anything you could find to make an honest buck. We children kept giving our father our earnings until we were of marriageable age."

Occasionally, an employer who valued the young immigrant's service gave him valuable advice. An Armenian boy whose widowed mother encouraged him to master a trade learned, while repairing a car, that he could study engineering for free at a night school on the MIT campus. Vozchan Parsegian would eventually earn a doctorate in nuclear physics and become the first dean of engineering at the Rensselaer Polytechnic Institute.

The orphaned John Alabilikian worked as an auto mechanic for a man who encouraged him to set up his own shop. "Anything you want from my shop—my advice, my tools—don't hesitate," he told the young immigrant. John reflected, "That's how much he liked me." And Chinese immigrant John Lui was introduced to an American family "who took me in and treated me like a son. I cleaned house and cooked for them and washed dishes. They gave me the key to the house, so I could do anything I liked. I wanted some pocket money and to save some money, so I became a shoe shine boy on weekends."

Immigrant Children Then and Now: Achievements, Aspirations, and Well-Being

Surveys of immigrant children whose families came to the United States since the 1980s report findings that are in striking agreement with the retrospective accounts of immigrants who came as children during the first half of the twentieth century. The most important study of more than 5,000 children of immigrants, conducted in 1992 by sociologists Alejandro Portes and Ruben Rumbaut, focused on fourteen- and fifteen-year-olds in two key areas of current immigrant settlement: Southern California and south Florida. The sample in San Diego included more than 2,400 Mexican, Filipino, Vietnamese, Cambodian, Laotian, and Hmong students. The sample in the Miami and Fort Lauderdale areas totaled about 2,800 Columbian, Cuban, Haitian, Nicaraguan, Jamaican, and West Indian students.[4]

The samples were equally split by grade level (eighth and ninth) and by gender. Fifty-six percent were foreign-born youths who immigrated to the United States before age twelve (the 1.5 generation), and 44 percent were U.S.-born children of immigrant parents (the second generation). Among the foreign-born children, the sample was evenly split by age of arrival. About half were preschool age at arrival, and the other half had reached elementary school age in their native country.

Regardless of their country of origin and their place of residence in the United States, immigrant children worked harder than their native-born classmates, spent more time on homework, got better grades, and dropped out of school far less often. Girls had significantly higher grade point averages and greater educational aspirations than the boys did.

A low level of parent-child conflict and a high level of social support by parents, by members of the extended family, and by competent peers who were of the same ethnic group were consistently associated with high achievement, high aspirations, high self-esteem, and low levels of depression among the children of immigrants. So was their fluency in English.

Lower parent-child conflict was also associated with higher parental education in smaller and more economically stable two-parent households. The human capital of parents and the social capital of family relationships gave immigrant children a significant advantage while adapting to their new country.

Two other large-scale studies that deal with the correlates of high achievement and psychological well-being among immigrant children utilized data from the National Longitudinal Study of Adolescent Health, a nationally representative study of adolescents in seventh through twelfth grades. One study, based on a sample of approximately 13,350 students, found that first-generation immigrants reported significantly less depression and greater positive well-being in adolescence than their native-born age-mates of similar demographic background.[5] Among protective factors that enabled the immigrant youths to maintain higher levels of psychological well-being were parental supervision, closeness with parents, lack of parent-child conflict, church attendance, the importance of religion and frequent prayer in their lives, and the social support that they received from family members, friends, and teachers.

A second study was based on a random sample of interviews with 5,002 children of U.S. natives and 635 immigrant children (mean age of sixteen). Children of Asian and Latino immigrants tended to outperform children of the native born. Extra-familial institutions, notably religious institutions, made a significant positive impact on their school achievement.[6]

A five-year, interdisciplinary Longitudinal Immigrant Student Adaptation Study (LISA), directed by Carola Suàrez-Oroczo and Marcel Suàrez-Oroczo, reports similar findings. The LISA study followed some 400 immigrant children (ages nine to fourteen at the beginning of the study) who came from five regions (China, Central America, the Dominican Republic, Haiti, and Mexico) to the Boston and San Francisco areas.[7]

Qualitative interview data and quantitative survey data employed in the LISA study illustrated both the importance of supportive friends, counselors, and members of the extended family in the social worlds of immigrant youths and the protective role of religion and church-based relationships in the lives of immigrant teenagers.

The role of protective factors in the lives of immigrant children has also been a major focus of the Kauai Longitudinal Study. For more than four decades, my colleagues and I have followed the development of a cohort of 698 individuals of Polynesian and Southeast Asian descent who were born in 1955 on the Hawaiian island of Kauai. About a third of our study's participants were children of Filipino immigrants. Their parents had little education, worked in unskilled jobs on the sugar and pineapple plantations, and lived in poverty. To our surprise, most of these children grew up to be competent, confident, and caring adults.[8]

We examined the protective factors that accounted for their resilience at five developmental stages: early and middle childhood, adolescence, young adulthood, and midlife. Among resources in the family and community that were associated with successful coping in these "high-risk" individuals were: maternal competence, close bonds with a primary caregiver, supportive siblings and grandparents, competent peer friends, supportive teachers, elder mentors, successful school experiences, and membership in youth clubs and church groups.

In the face of serious adversities, the resilient children of Kauai relied on sources of support within their families and community that *increased* their competence and confidence, *decreased* the number of stressful life events they subsequently encountered, and *opened*

up new opportunities for them. Though the context of their departure and reception differed, the immigrant children who came
through Ellis and Angel islands followed a similar path and relied
on similar resources.

12

From Sojourners to Citizens

JOHN ALABILIKIAN, whose parents were killed in the 1915 massacre of the Armenians, considered himself lucky. His aunt and her Turkish husband adopted him, and he managed to get to the United States when he was fourteen years old. Sixty years later, he remembered:

> When I saw the Statue of Liberty, I thought I was in heaven. She is up there and saying, "Come on in. From now on you are a free person. You can do as you please. And as long as you be- have yourself, you are coming to a country where you can make a success—it's up to you." That's the first thing you see when you come to this country. So I want to thank America. I want to thank the Constitution that gave us all of this.

Given a chance, no one is more patriotic than a new immigrant. When asked how they felt about America, the men and women who came through Ellis Island and Angel Island as children—regardless of their countries of origin—were invariably enthusiastic about their adopted country. The pattern of their lives, which had evolved over time, was congruent with the motto of the Great Seal of the United States, *E Pluribus Unum*. Out of many, they had became one.

Naturalization is a slow process, but with only a few exceptions, the immigrant children were eager to learn English and to become American citizens. The moment they began to say "we" rather than "they," they graduated from being sojourners to being members of "a unique country that stands for something special in the world."[1]

Remembered JOHANNA FLAHERTY from Ireland,

> I wanted to become a citizen right away. The first thing I wanted to learn was the Pledge of Allegiance and the "Star Spangled Banner." . . . I asked eight of the girls who worked with me, "Will you please write me the words of the national anthem," but not one of them could write it. . . . I finally got it in a box of Fannie Farmer's candy. It was on the inside, the national anthem and the flag.

DORA ESSEL from Germany wanted to become a citizen as soon as she turned twenty-one years old:

> I wanted to be able to vote. I went to night school and studied the history of this country. At the time of our citizenship exams, we sat in front of a judge, and he asked questions about the first thirteen states, about Congress, about our representatives and senators, and about some of the early presidents. I think we learned more about this country than some people who were born here. When we got our papers, it was a happy day. There were some twenty-five of us who were sworn in as new citizens, and I felt like an American right then and there. When you got your papers, you knew you belonged here.

ESTHER BLATT, daughter of Holocaust survivors and born in a DP camp, studied hard with her mother for the citizenship tests.

> I can picture her: she is ironing, and I am reading the questions to her. How many stripes are in the flag and what do they represent? How many members are there in the House of Representatives? It was a somber occasion when we went in front of the judge and I got my own citizenship papers, together with my parents.

Oreste Teglia from Italy waited a long time—some twenty years—to become a citizen, "but I was happy when I did it. I felt like an American. . . . It meant an awful lot to me to be able to be in this country. Whatever I have achieved here wouldn't have been possible in Europe."

Like her fellow countrymen, Sandy Loretta Lococo Mazza appreciated the chance to make friends with many different kinds of people. "What I love about America is that everyone is on one level [before the law]. Everybody can be friends with everybody else. [In] Italy . . . they haven't got tolerance for a lot of things you find here. I am a very lucky person to live here."

As a Polish-Jewish immigrant child growing up in the Bronx, Kate Simon valued "the watching, the listening, the learning of phrases, the tremendous awareness at all times, and a certain kind of responsiveness to all people. That is part of the immigration thing, the sense of mingling with Americans that fosters curiosity rather than xenophobia."

And Esther Blatt treasured the fact "that I have this very rich history to draw from, coming as an immigrant myself. It makes you different from everybody else but not in a negative way. I always hope that I can make people understand what the immigrant experience was like and what it means to be an American —a proud, wonderful thing to be."

Emmi Kremer paid tribute to the kindness of the strangers she encountered: "I have had so many people along the way help me. There is so much good here in America, if you only look around and reach out. I am still reaching out. I am still trying."

Immigrant children, especially those "unaccompanied minors" who came alone—and whose ranks are on the rise today—appreciated that kindness. They were grateful for the help provided by those volunteers who assisted them when they arrived at their point of debarkation; the train conductors who saw to it that they reached their point of destination; the sponsors who provided a job and housing; the neighbors who taught them how to change money, how to shop, and how to find a bargain when money was scarce; and the nurses who took care of them in detention when they were sick and frightened.

Unique among these kind strangers was Katherine Maurer, a Methodist deaconess from San Francisco who worked at the Angel

Island Immigration Station. The Chinese detainees called her Kuan Yin ("goddess of mercy") for her good works during twenty-eight of the thirty years of the immigration station's life. In addition to English lessons, she provided toiletries, clothing, and toys for the children, and helped some of the teenage detainees get jobs, once they left Angel Island. She also organized Christmas parties for the detainees just as volunteers at Ellis Island did.

Once they became citizens, the immigrant children repaid the kindness of strangers in many ways. They sent CARE packages to the hungry in war-torn Europe and money and clothing to countries, like Latvia, that had been liberated after World War II. They paid for the college education of relatives left behind in Europe, and they salvaged the remnants of the cultural heritage of countries, like Armenia, that had become newly independent after the Cold War and the Soviet Union's dissolution.

They also became mentors for the new immigrants who arrived in the United States. Said SALLY KLEINMAN GURIAN, a Jew who had immigrated as a child from Russia:

> When I grew up my parents wanted a better life for us. We loved being here. We were happy here, and we remembered that we had nobody to teach us unless we went to school and learned. So my daughter and I taught immigrants at the International Center.
>
> We taught adults and teenagers who didn't know any English. And we taught Cambodian children who had come over here. We taught them English, we took them out and played games with them, and we had books for them. We tried to sort of pay back what our American teachers had done for us.

In the closing chapter of her book *Small Strangers*, which deals with the experiences of immigrant children in an earlier ear (1880–1925), Melissa Klapper concludes that "the specific cast of characters has changed, but . . . the social script has not. . . . Now, as then, various forms of education are the prime mediators of most immigrant children's formative experiences in America."[2]

Scholars of migration and education have repeatedly taken note of these children's unusual success in school. The anthropologists John Ogbu and Margaret Gibson observed that when young immigrants know that, as a result of their migration, their opportunities are greater than those in their countries of origin, they take advantage of the education they are offered even if it is in poor neighborhoods with dilapidated schools.[3] That observation was true for the Jewish children who came from Russia and Poland and studied in crowded classrooms in the Bronx, for Swedish children who learned English in a one-room schoolhouse in rural North Dakota, and for the Chinese "paper sons" who lived and studied in San Francisco's congested Chinatown.

The immigrant children turned into ambitious and hard-working students because they came with a sense of purpose and an awareness of the potential opportunities that came with schooling. They learned to appreciate the golden opportunity of the free public education the United States offered. A cursory look at some of these children's records attests to the transforming power of that education:

There is ten-year-old Edward Corsi from Italy who landed in New York in 1907, studied English in a settlement house, obtained a law degree from Fordham University, and was appointed Commissioner of Immigration at Ellis Island twenty-four years after he first arrived on American soil.

There is peripatetic Kate Simon who arrived in 1918 as a four-year-old from Warsaw. She loved the books she could check out (for free!) in the public library, became an accomplished travel writer, and chronicled her life as an immigrant child growing up in the Bronx.

There is twelve-year-old Edward Rune Myrbeck, a Swedish orphan, who came to the United States in 1923 and was called "Square Head" by the children in his Illinois classroom. After a lifetime of accomplishment in the electronics industry, he was knighted by the king of Sweden for his service to his native country.

There is nine-year-old Emmi Kremer who emigrated in 1926 from Germany. She loved school and books and wrote poetry and songs about the American flag and the Statue of Liberty. In retirement she became the unofficial poet of Ellis Island.

There is John Lui, a Chinese "paper son" who at age twelve arrived in San Francisco in 1936, attended public schools, and became a top-notch aircraft mechanic during World War II. He fixed the engines for the B-29 plane that dropped the atomic bomb on Japan.

And there is Arno Penzias, a seven-year-old Jewish refugee from Munich who went to England aboard a Kindertransport and then sailed to New York in January 1940. Educated in the public schools in the Bronx, the City College of New York, and Columbia University, he became a radio astronomer at Bell Laboratories in New Jersey. Thirty-nine years after he set foot on American soil, he received the Nobel Prize in Physics.

A leading historian of childhood, Paula Fass, suggests that children can often be a driving force in a family's migration and adaptation to a new country since they tend to be optimistic and hopeful about the future.[4] As we have seen in their oral histories, immigrant children become "translators" at the margin between cultures and generations, the past and the future.

The children from Ellis Island and Angel Island were not passive "victims" of the immigration experience. Instead, they became adept at actively shaping their new environment. They found opportunities for social mobility through education and jobs that would make life easier for their own sons and daughters and their grandchildren as well. They were remarkably resilient and resourceful, even during periods of economic depression and war and despite prevailing prejudices against the newcomers that took the form of "No [Chinese/Irish/Italians/Jews] need apply."

Their labor contributed to the unprecedented productivity and economic growth of their new country. Their service in the armed forces during World War II and the Korean War was exemplary. Many, including the women, volunteered. Thyra Pearson from Sweden, for instance, joined the WAAC. The Chinese "paper sons" also served their new country honorably: Benjamin Choy built victory ships for the Department of Defense, John Lui joined the U.S. Army Air Force after the Japanese attack on Pearl Harbor, and Hop Jeong was in a military intelligence unit during the Korean War.

The men and women who came through Ellis Island when they were children remained active throughout their lives, even when they reached the age of retirement. Several of the women who were interviewed in their seventies worked in senior centers in their communities. Said seventy-seven-year-old Kathleen Harlow from Great Britain, "I still do a lot of volunteer work. . . . I can look back and say I had a very productive life. . . . I can do pretty much what I want to do, and nobody stops me. I still get excited when the sun comes up!"

Eighty-one-year-old Rose Siegal Alber Levine from Russia also worked as a volunteer at her local Senior Center, serving lunches and doing arts and crafts. "I had a full life. It wasn't always an easy life, but I love America." Seventy-nine-year-old Liesel Rubin Saretzky from Austria every day strove "to make the world a little better. I make quilts for the Make-A-Wish Foundation and volunteer with underprivileged African American children."

And seventy-two-year-old Clara Honold from Germany, though officially retired, continued to expand her progressive experimental school. "I am very American, but I cannot overlook the fact that I had such a marvelous [educational] heritage. I must share this with others and pass it on."

And when Arno Penzias moved from Bell Laboratories' in New Jersey to California's Silicon Valley, to the primary incubator of tiny start-up enterprises, he surprised everyone. At age seventy-two he wrote, "I hit upon the idea of turning what I had been enjoying most into a full-time job: helping to shape new ideas and bringing them to practical fruition. . . . Needless to say, I have no plans to retire."

Vozchan Parsegian *did* retire from his position as dean of engineering at the Rensselaer Polytechnic Institute to take on a twenty-year project—without a salary—to preserve the monuments of his native Armenia. This project produced forty-two thousand images and seven volumes on the architecture of some 940 sites that can be found at more than a hundred major research libraries in Europe, the United States, and Canada. "That has been something that we have been very pleased about," he said. At age eighty-six, he reflected on the moral code that stayed with him throughout his life: "My mother taught us, 'Just do your best, just do your best.'"

That motto reflects the legacy of the other child immigrants as well—they *did* their best. They acquired the skills and competencies needed to become productive members of their adopted country. They worked hard, often in jobs that native-born Americans were reluctant to take, and they never lost their optimism about a future that would give their children an opportunity to be better educated and to enjoy a better life than they had known when they were young.

They also shared strong family ties and turned to members of their extended family for financial and emotional support when needed. They cherished teachers, mentors, members of their community of faith, and kind strangers who opened up doors of opportunity for them and showed them, by example, what America is all about.

The twenty-first-century waves of immigration involve children from different cultural backgrounds than the children who arrived at Ellis and Angel islands in the first half of the twentieth century. Beneath the surface differences, however, they share similar values: the importance of family ties, an emphasis on hard work, and optimism about the future.[5]

In her essay "What It Means to Be American in the 21st Century," Tamar Jacoby offers a definition that readily applies to all the children of immigrants who come to our shores:

> What it means to be American is essentially to arrive as a newcomer—to start over and make a new life. From the Pilgrims . . . to the Ellis Island generation, this is the one experience that all Americans share; this and what follows—finding a way to fit in or hang together . . . by balancing your particularity against the common culture that accrued over time.[6]

"The civic principles we share," suggests Amitai Etzioni, include "a commitment to the Constitution, the Bill of Rights, and the democratic form of government; a general respect for the law; English as the shared language; mutual respect for people who are different; and some shared notion of morality."[7]

That civics lesson of a lifetime was what the children of Ellis Island and Angel Island learned. It is a lesson as timely today as it was in 1921, when eleven-year-old Rose Levine, newly arrived from Russia, urged her nine-year-old brother, "Come, come, let's look around America!"

Appendix A:
Child Immigrants to the United States, 1892–1954

Between 1892 and 1954, approximately 3.4 million children immigrated to the United States.

Year	# of Children	Year	# of Children
1892	89,167	1924	132,264
1893	57,392	1925	50,722
1894	41,755	1926	47,347
1895	33,289	1927	51,689
1896	52,741	1928	49,680
1897	38,627	1929	47,935
1898	38,267	1930	40,777
1899	43,983	1931	17,320
1900	54,624	1932	6,781
1901	62,562	1933	4,131
1902	74,063	1934	5,389
1903	102,431	1935	6,893
1904	109,150	1936	6,925
1905	114,668	1937	8,326
1906	136,273	1938	10,181
1907	138,344	1939	12,204
1908	112,148	1940	9,602
1909	88,393	1941	7,982
1910	120,509	1942	3,710
1911	117,837	1943	3,179
1912	113,700	1944	4,092
1913	147,158	1945	5,645
1914	158,621	1946	11,092
1915	52,982	1947	18,831
1916	47,070	1948	24,095
1917	47,467	1949	32,728
1918	21,349	1950	50,468
1919	26,373	1951	44,023
1920	81,890	1952	64,513
1921	146,613	1953	37,016
1922	63,710	1954	45,105
1923	91,816		

Source: Moreno, *Children of Ellis Island*, 125.

Appendix B: Selected Chronology
Changes in U.S. Immigration and Naturalization Laws

The entries listed here were selected from James Crawford's hand-out for the National Immigration Forum to provide a context for the case studies discussed in the text, as does the table Child Immigrants to the United States (1892–1954), from Barry Moreno.

1790—Naturalization is authorized for "free white persons" who have resided in the United States for at least two years and swear loyalty to the U.S. Constitution. The racial requirement would remain on the federal books until 1952, although naturalization was opened to certain Asian nationalities in the 1940s.

1798—The *Alien and Sedition Acts* authorize the president to deport any foreigner deemed to be dangerous and make it a crime to speak, write, or publish anything "of a false, scandalous, and malicious nature" about the president or Congress. An amended *Naturalization Act* imposes a fourteen-year residency requirement for prospective citizens; in 1802, Congress reduces the waiting period to five years, a provision that remains today.

1819—*Reporting Rule* adopted. Data begin to be collected on immigration into the United States. Ships' captains and others are required to keep and submit manifests of immigrants entering the United States.

1882–1943—The *Chinese Exclusion Act* restricts immigration by Chinese to native-born U.S. citizens, diplomats, merchants, and students; suspends immigration by Chinese laborers. This marks the first time the United States has restricted immigration on the basis of race or national origin.

1892—Ellis Island opens. Between 1892 and 1954, more than 12 million immigrants will be processed at this one facility.

1906—The *first language requirement* is adopted for naturalization: the ability to speak and understand English.

1910—Angel Island Immigration Station opens. Between 1910 and 1940 over one million people come here from accross the Pacific Rim.

1921—A new form of immigration restriction is born: *the national-origins quota system.* Admissions from each European country will be limited to 3 percent of each foreign-born nationality in the 1910 census. The effect is to favor northern Europeans at the expense of southern and eastern Europeans. Immigration from Western Hemisphere nations remains unrestricted; most Asians will continue to face exclusion.

1927—*Immigration ceiling further reduced.* The annual immigration ceiling is further reduced to 150,000; the quota is revised to 2 percent of each nationality's representation in the 1920 census. The basic law remains in effect through 1965.

1929—*National Origins Act.* The annual immigration ceiling of 150,000 is made permanent, with 70 percent of admissions slated for those coming from northern and western Europe while the other 30 percent are reserved for those coming from southern and eastern Europe.

1948—*Displaced Persons Act.* Entry is allowed for 400,000 persons displaced by World War II. However, such refugees must pass a security check and have proof of employment and housing that does not threaten U.S. citizens' jobs and homes.

1965—The United States finally *eliminates racial criteria* from its immigration laws. Each country, regardless of ethnicity, will receive an annual quota of 20,000, under a ceiling of 170,000.

1980—*Refugee Act.* A system is developed to handle refugees as a class separate from other immigrants. Under the new law, refugees are defined as those who flee a country because of persecution "on account of race, religion, nationality, or political opinion." The president, in consultation with Congress, is authorized to establish an annual ceiling on the number of refugees who may enter the United States. The president also is allowed to admit any group of refugees in an emergency. At the same time, the annual ceiling on traditional immigration is raised to 270,000.

Source: Prepared by James Crawford for the National Immigration Forum, 2003.

Notes

Introduction
1. Barry Moreno, *Children of Ellis Island* (Charleston, SC: Arcadia Publishing, 2005).
2. Barry Moreno, *Encyclopedia of Ellis Island* (Westport, CT: Greenwood Press, 2004).
3. Aaron K. DiFranco and Kella de Castro Svetich, eds., *Conversations between Generations: Stories from the Angel Island Oral History Project* (Davis, CA: University of California–Davis, Pacific Regional Humanities Center, 2006).
4. Charles Hirschman, "Immigration and the American Century," *Demography* 42, no. 4 (November 2005): 595–620.

Chapter 1: Passing Through Ellis Island
1. Philip M. Hoose, *We Were There, Too! Young People in U.S. History* (New York: Farrar Straus Giroux, 2001); and Robert H. Bremmer, ed., *Children and Youth in America: A Documentary History*, vol. 1, *1600–1865* (Cambridge, MA: Harvard University Press, 1970).
2. Susan Arrington Madsen, *I Walked to Zion: True Stories of Young Pioneers on the Mormon Trail* (Salt Lake City, UT: Desert Book Company, 1994).
3. Moreno, "Introduction," in *Encyclopedia of Ellis Island*.
4. Bertha M. Boody, *A Psychological Study of Immigrant Children at Ellis Island* (Baltimore: Williams and Wilkins, 1926).
5. Moreno, *Children of Ellis Island*.

Chapter 2: First in Line: Child Immigrants from the British Isles

1. Sam Roberts, "Story of the First through Ellis Island Is Rewritten," *New York Times*, September 14, 2006, A1, 24; and Sam Roberts, "A Great-Great-Great-Great Day for Annie," *New York Times*, September 15, 2006.
2. Peter Morton Coan, *Ellis Island Interviews: In Their Own Words* (New York: Barnes & Noble, 2004), 75, 105, 131, 139.
3. Kathleen Eason Harlow, interview, May 18, 1993. Interviewer: Janet Levine (Ellis Island Oral History Project). (All subsequent interviews in this chapter come from the Ellis Island Oral History Project.)
4. Eleanor Ruth Kenderline Lenhart, interview, September 5, 1985. Interviewer: Dana Gumb.
5. Johanna Flaherty, interview, May 29, 1986. Interviewer: Debra Allen.
6. Donald Roberts, interview, August 15, 1985. Interviewer: Edward Applebome.
7. Anne Reilly Quinn, interview, December 8, 1983. Interviewers: Dennis Cloutier and Peter Kaplan.

Chapter 3: From the Pale of Settlement to the Golden Land

1. Moreno, "Hebrew Immigrant Aid Society," in *Encyclopedia of Ellis Island*, 105.
2. Sadie Guttman Kaplan, interview, July 2, 1992. Interviewer: Paul E. Sigrist, Jr. (Ellis Island Oral History Project). (All subsequent interviews in this chapter come from the Ellis Island Oral History Project.)
3. Irving Halperin, interview, May 24, 1989. Interviewer: Andrew Phillips.
4. Sally (Surka) Kleinman Gurian, interview, September 27, 1991. Interviewer: Janet Levine.
5. Celia Adler, interview, November 21, 1985. Interviewer: Debby Dane.
6. Kate Simon, interview, June 2, 1986. Interviewer: Nancy Dallett.
7. Harry Singer (Girschkov Zingerman), interview, June 26, 1992. Interviewer: Janet Levine.
8. Rose Siegal Alber Levine, interview, August 20, 1991. Interviewer: Paul E. Sigrist, Jr.

Chapter 4: The Italian Bambini

1. Moreno, "Races and Peoples," in *Encyclopedia of Ellis Island*, 200.
2. Edward Corsi, *In the Shadow of Liberty: The Chronicle of Ellis Island* (New York: Macmillan, 1935).
3. Oreste Teglia, interview, December 20, 1985. Interviewer: Debra Dane (Ellis Island Oral History Project). (All subsequent interviews in this chapter come from the Ellis Island Oral History Project.)
4. Marion Da Ronca, interview, February 25, 1992. Interviewer: Paul E. Sigrist, Jr.

5. Annette Terlizzi Monouydas, interview, April 24, 1995. Interviewer: Paul E. Sigrist, Jr.
6. Rita Costa Finco, interview, December 31, 1996. Interviewer: Janet Levine.
7. Sunday (Domenica) Calabresa Wood, interview, March 25, 1992. Interviewer: Janet Levine.
8. Sandy (Santa) Loretta Lococo Mazza, interview, December 28, 1996. Interviewer: Janet Levine.

Chapter 5: St. Olaf's Children from Scandinavia
1. Coan, *Ellis Island Interviews*, 339.
2. Thyra Pearson, interview, December 17, 1985. Interviewer: Nancy Dallett (Ellis Island Oral History Project). (All subsequent interviews in this chapter come from the Ellis Island Oral History Project.)
3. Edward Rune Myrbeck Sr., interview, February, 4, 1986. Interviewer: Debby Dane.
4. Martha Hoglind, interview, April 17, 1993. Interviewer: Janet Levine.
5. Asta M. Andersen Hoglind, interview, April 17, 1993. Interviewer: Janet Levine.
6. Ingrid Ahlfors, interview, February 5, 1986. Interviewer: Nancy Dallett.

Chapter 6: Survivors of the Armenian Genocide
1. Robert P. Jordan, "The Proud Armenians," *National Geographic*, June 1978, 846–73.
2. Donald E. Miller and Lorna Touryan Miller, *Survivors: An Oral History of the Armenian Genocide* (Berkeley: University of California Press, 1993), 18–24.
3. Vozchan Parsegian (Hovsepian), interview, July 11, 1994. Interviewer: Paul E. Sigrist, Jr. (Ellis Island Oral History Project). (All subsequent interviews in this chapter come from the Ellis Island Oral History Project.)
4. Albert Miamidian and Satina Papazian, interview, October 23, 1985. Interviewer: Nancy Dallett.
5. Ervanthouhi Garabidian Assadourian, interview, May 26, 1993. Interviewer: Janet Levine.
6. Vartan Hartunian, interview, February 3, 1986. Interviewer: Debby Dane. Excerpts from interviews with his three older sisters are reprinted in Coan, *Ellis Island Interviews*, 402–6.
7. John Alabilikian, interview, October 23, 1985. Interviewer: Nancy Dallett.

Chapter 7: German Immigrant Children During the Great Depression
1. William L. Shirer, *The Rise and Fall of the Third Reich: A History of Nazi Germany* (New York: Simon & Schuster, 1960), 95–97 (in Crest Print edition, 1962).
2. Inge Nastke, interview, February 6, 1986. Interviewer: Edward

Applebome (Ellis Island Oral History Project). (All subsequent interviews in this chapter come from the Ellis Island Oral History Project.)

3. Dora Essel, interview, November 20, 1985. Interviewer: Debbie Dane.

4. Emmi Tegeler Kremer, interview, January 23, 1996. Interviewer: Janet Levine.

5. Clara Honold, interview, April 20, 1993. Interviewer: Janet Levine.

Chapter 8: Escape from Hitler's Third Reich

1. Shirer. *Rise and Fall of the Third Reich,* 323, 477–78, 580–82 (in Crest Print edition).

2. Wolfgang Benz, "Emigration as Rescue and Trauma: The Historical Context of the Kindertransport," *Shofar* 23 (Fall 2004).

3. Bertha Leverton and Shmuel Loewenson, eds., *I Came Alone: The Stories of the Kindertransports* (Sussex, UK: Book Guild, 1998).

4. Philip K. Jason and Iris Posner, eds., *Don't Wave Goodbye: The Children's Flight from Nazi Persecution to American Freedom* (Westport, CT: Praeger, 2004).

5. Harry Hochstadt, interview, December 8, 1993. Interviewer: Janet Levine.

6. Lisa (Liesl) Rubin Saretzky, interview, February 13, 2004. Interviewer: Janet Levine (Ellis Island Oral History Project).

7. Arno Penzias, Autobiography, http://nobelprize.Org/nobel_prizes/physics/laureates/1978/penzias-autobio.html (Nobel Foundation, June 2005).

8. Fred Cige, interview, August 13, 2004. Interviewer: Janet Levine (Ellis Island Oral History Project).

Chapter 9: Europe's Displaced Children Come to the United States

1. Marc Wyman, *DPs: Europe's Displaced Persons, 1945–1951* (Ithaca, NY: Cornell University Press, 1998).

2. "549 More DPs Land after Rough Trip," *New York Times,* December 22, 1948, 14.

3. Esther Blatt, interview, March 5, 2004. Interviewer: Janet Levine (Ellis Island Oral History Project).

4. Ilze Jatnieks-Grotans, Michelle Klees Papers, Immigration History Research Center (IHRC) 1223, Box 1, Folder 10, University of Minnesota, Minneapolis.

5. Girts Jatnieks, Michelle Klees Papers, IHRC 1223, Box l, Folder l.

6. Gunda Grotans-Luss, Michelle Klees Papers, IHRC 1223, Box 1, Folder 8.

7. Janis Skujins, Michelle Klees Papers, IHRC 1223, Box 1, Folder 4; and Michelle Klees, "Persevering Endurance: Latvia to Minnesota," graduate thesis, University of Northern Colorado, Greeley, May 2002.

Chapter 10: The Paper Sons of Angel Island

1. Coan, *Ellis Island Interviews,* 417.

2. Erika Lee, *At America's Gates: Chinese Immigration during the Exclusion*

Era, 1882–1943 (Chapel Hill: University of North Carolina Press, 2003), 75, 207; and Robert Barde and Gustavo J. Bobonis, "Detention at Angel Island: First Empirical Evidence," *Social Science History* 30 (Spring 2006): 103–36.

3. Valerie Natale, "Angel Island: Guardian of the Western Gate," *Prologue*, Summer 1998, 128–29.

4. Ibid., 129–31.

5. Him, Mark Lai, Genny Lim, and Judy Yung, *Island: Poetry and History of Chinese Immigrants on Angel Island, 1910–1940* (Seattle: University of Washington Press, 1991), 110–11.

6. Benjamin Choy, Angel Island Oral History (AIOH) Project, Pacific Regional Humanities Center, University of California–Davis, Paper AIOH-3, 2004.

7. James Louie in "History Corner—Oral History: Two Tales of Angel Island," *Passages: The Newsletter of the Angel Island Immigration Station Foundation* 5, no. 1 (Fall 2001): 4.

8. Albert Kai Wong, "A Child's Eye View of Angel Island Immigration Station," interview by Adam Wimbush, 2000, in *The Newsletter of The Angel Island Immigration Station Foundation*; and Katrina Saltonstall Currier, *Kai's Journey to Gold Mountain: An Angel Island Story* (Tiburon, CA: Angel Island Association, 2005).

9. John Lui, AIOH Project, Pacific Regional Humanities Center, University of California–Davis, Paper AIOH-A, 2004.

10. Hop Jeong, AIOH Project, Pacific Regional Humanities Center, University of California–Davis, Paper AIOH-21, 2006; and Milly Lee, *Landed* (New York: Farrar Straus Giroux, 2006).

11. Myron Ning Wong in DiFranco and de Castro Svetich, *Conversations between Generations*, 11–12, 22, 26, 45–46.

12. Lee, *At America's Gates*, 251; and Branwell Fanning and William Wong, *Angel Island* (Charleston, SC: Arcadia Publishing, 2006), 128.

Chapter 11: Risk and Protective Factors in the Lives of Immigrant Children

1. Carola Suàrez-Orozco, "Immigrant Families and Their Children: Adaptation and Identity Formation," in *The Blackwell Companion to Sociology*, ed. Judith R. Blau (Malden, MA: Blackwell, 2001), 128–39.

2. Robert N. Butler, "The Life Review: An Interpretation of Reminiscence in the Aged," in *New Thoughts on Old Age*, ed. Robert Kastenbaum (New York: Springer, 1964), 265–80.

3. Donald A. Ritchie, *Doing Oral History: A Practical Guide* (New York: Oxford University Press, 2003), 33.

4. Ruben Rumbaut, "Ties That Bind," in *Immigration and the Family: Research and Policy on U.S. Immigrants*, eds. Alan Booth, Ann C. Crouter, and Nancy Landale (Mahwah, NJ: Lawrence Erlbaum Associates, 1997), 28–40.

5. Kathryn Harker, "Immigrant Generation, Assimilation, and Adolescent Psychological Well-Being," *Social Forces* 79 (2001): 969–1004.

6. Carl L. Bankston III and Min Zhou, "Social Capital and Immigrant Children's Achievement," *Sociology of Education* 13 (2002): 13–39.

7. Carola Suàrze-Orozco and Irina L. G. Todorova, "The Social Worlds of Immigrant Youth," *New Directions for Youth Development* 100 (Winter 2003): 15–24; Nora E. Thompson and Andrea G. Gurney, "He Is Everything: Religion's Role in the Lives of Immigrant Youth," *New Directions for Youth Development* 100 (Winter 2003): 75–90; and Desirée Baolian Qin-Hilliard, "Gendered Expectation and Gendered Experiences: Immigrant Students' Adaptation in Schools," *New Directions for Youth Development* 100 (Winter 2003): 91–109.

8. Emmy E. Werner and Ruth S. Smith, *Journeys from Childhood to Midlife: Risk, Resilience, and Recovery* (Ithaca: NY: Cornell University Press, 2001).

Chapter 12: From Sojourners to Citizens

1. Tamar Jacoby, "The New Immigrants: A Progress Report," in *Reinventing the Melting Pot: The New Immigrants and What It Means to Be American* (New York: Basic Books, 2004), 27.

2. Melissa R. Klapper, *Small Strangers: The Experiences of Immigrant Children, 1880–1925* (Chicago: Ivan R. Dee, 2007), 181.

3. Margaret A. Gibson and John U. Ogbu, eds., *Minority Status and Schooling: A Comparative Study of Immigrant and Involuntary Minorities* (New York: Garland, 1991).

4. Paula S. Fass, "Children in Global Migrations," *Journal of Social History,* Summer 2005, 948–49.

5. Carola Suàrez-Orozco and Marcelo M. Suàrez-Orozco, *Children of Immigration* (Cambridge, MA: Harvard University Press, 2001), 158.

6. Tamar Jacoby, "What It Means to Be American in the 21st Century," in *Reinventing the Melting Pot,* 313.

7. Amitai Etzioni, "Diversity within Unity," in *Reinventing the Melting Pot,* 220.

Bibliography

Alba, Richard D., and others. *The Immigrant Experience for Families and Children.* Washington, DC: American Sociological Association, 1999.

Antin, Mary. *At School in the Promised Land or the Story of a Little Immigrant.* Boston: Houghton Mifflin, 1912.

———. *The Promised Land.* Boston: Houghton Mifflin, 1912.

Bankston, Carl L., III, and Min Zhou. "Social Capital and Immigrant Children's Achievement." *Sociology of Education* 13 (2002): 13–39.

Berger, Roni, and Tzipi Weiss. "Immigration and Posttraumatic Growth—a Missing Link." *Journal of Immigrant and Refugee Services* 1, no. 2 (2002): 21–39.

Berrol, Selma Cantor. *Growing Up American: Immigrant Children in America, Then and Now.* New York: Twayne, 1995.

———. "Immigrant Children at School." In *The Social Fabric: American Life from the Civil War to the Present,* edited by John H. Cary and others. New York: Longman, 1999.

Bolino, August C. *The Ellis Island Source Book.* Washington, DC: Kensington Historical Press, 1985.

171

Boody, Bertha M. *A Psychological Study of Immigrant Children at Ellis Island.* Baltimore: Williams and Wilkins, 1926.

Booth, Alan, Ann C. Crouter, and Nancy Landale, eds. *Immigration and the Family: Research and Policy on U.S. Immigrants.* Part II: "How Does Migration Experience Affect Child and Adolescent Development?" Mahwah, NJ: Lawrence Erlbaum, 1997.

Brandon, Peter David. "The Living Arrangements of Children in Immigrant Families in the United States." *International Migration Review* 38 (2002): 416–36.

Bunting, Eve. *Dreaming of America: An Ellis Island Story.* Mahwah, NJ: Bridgewater Books, 2000.

Card, D., J. DiNardo, and E. Estes. "The More Things Change: Immigrants and the Children of Immigrants in the 1940's, the 1970's, and the 1990's." Cambridge, MA: National Bureau of Economic Research, Working Paper 6519, April 1998.

Coan, Peter Morton. *Ellis Island Interviews: In Their Own Words.* New York: Barnes & Noble, 2004.

Cohen, Rose (Gallup). *Out of the Shadow.* Ithaca, NY: Cornell University Press, 1995; originally published in 1918 by George H. Doran Company.

Coli, Cynthia Garcia, and Katherine Magnuson. "The Psychological Experience of Immigration: A Developmental Perspective." In Booth, Crouter, and Landale, *Immigration and the Family,* 91–113.

Corsi, Edward. *In the Shadow of Liberty: The Chronicle of Ellis Island.* New York: Macmillan, 1935.

Covello, Leonard. *The Heart Is the Teacher.* With Guido D'Agostino. New York: McGraw Hill, 1958.

Currier, Katrina Saltonstall. *Kai's Journey to Gold Mountain: An Angel Island Story.* Tiburon, CA: Angel Island Association, 2005.

Daniels, Roger. *Coming to America: A History of Immigration and Ethnicity in American Life.* New York: Harper Collins/Perennial, 2000.

———. *Guarding the Golden Door: American Immigration Policy and Immigrants since 1882.* New York: Hill and Wang, 2004.

De Leon Siantz, Mary Lou. "Factors That Impact Developmental Outcomes of Immigrant Children." In Booth, Crouter, and Landale, *Immigration and the Family,* 149–61.

DiFranco, Aaron K., and Kella de Castro Svetich, eds. *Conversations between Generations: Stories from the Angel Island Oral History Project.* Davis, CA: University of California–Davis, Pacific Regional Humanities Center, 2006.

Drucker, Olga Levy. *Kindertransport.* New York: Henry Holt, 1992.

Dublin, Thomas, ed. *Immigrant Voices: New Lives in America, 1773–1986.* Urbana: University of Illinois Press, 1993.

Eltis, David, ed. *Coerced and Free Migration: Global Perspectives.* Stanford, CA: Stanford University Press, 2002.

Fass, Paula S. "Children in Global Migrations." *Journal of Social History,* Summer 2005, 937–50.

———. "Immigration and Education in the United States." In *Children of the New World: Society, Culture, and Globalization,* 23–48. New York: New York University Press, 2007.

Fass, Paula S., and Mary Ann Mason, eds. *Childhood in America.* New York: New York University Press, 2000.

Foner, Nancy. *From Ellis Island to JFK: New York's Two Great Waves of Immigration.* New Haven: Yale University Press, 2000.

Freedman, Russell. *Immigrant Kids.* New York: Dutton, 1980.

Fuligni, Andrew J. "A Comparative Longitudinal Approach to Acculturation among Children from Immigrant Families." *Harvard Educational Review* 71 (2001): 566–78.

Gibson, Margaret A., and John U. Ogbu, eds. *Minority Status and Schooling: A Comparative Study of Immigrant and Involuntary Minorities.* New York: Garland, 1991.

Glenn, Susan A. *Daughters of the Shtetl: Life and Labor in the Immigrant Generation.* Ithaca, NY: Cornell University Press, 1990.

Harker, Kathryn. "Immigrant Generation, Assimilation, and Adolescent Psychological Well-Being." *Social Forces* 79 (2001): 969–1004.

Hernandez, Donald J. "Demographic Change and the Life Circumstances of Immigrant Families." *The Future of Children* 14 (2004): 17–47.

Hirschman, Charles. "Immigration and the American Century." *Demography* 42, no. 4 (November 2005): 595–620.

Hoobler, Dorothy, and Thomas Hoobler. *We Are Americans: Voices of the Immigrant Experience.* New York: Scholastic, 2003.

Hoose, Phillip M. *We Were There, Too! Young People in U.S. History*. New York: Farrar Straus Giroux, 2001.

Hutner, Gordon, ed. *Immigrant Voices: Twenty-four Narratives on Becoming an American*. New York: Signet Books, 1999.

Igoa, Cristina. *The Inner World of the Immigrant Child*. New York: St. Martin's Press, 1995.

Illick, Joseph E. *American Childhoods*. Philadelphia: University of Pennsylvania Press, 2002.

Jacoby, Tamar, ed. *Reinventing the Melting Pot: The New Immigrants and What It Means to Be American*. New York: Basic Books, 2004.

Jason, Philip K., and Iris Posner, eds. *Don't Wave Goodbye: The Children's Flight from Nazi Persecution to American Freedom*. Westport, CT: Praeger, 2004.

Kao, G., and M. Tienda. "Optimism and Achievement: The Educational Performance of Immigrant Youth." *Social Science Quarterly* 76 (1995): 1–19.

Klapper, Melissa R. *Small Strangers: The Experiences of Immigrant Children in America, 1880–1925*. Chicago: Ivan R. Dee, 2007.

Lai, Him Mark, Genny Lim, and Judy Yung. *Island: Poetry and History of Chinese Immigrants on Angel Island, 1910–1940*. Seattle: University of Washington Press, 1991.

Lansford, Jennifer E., Kirby Deater-Deckard, and Marc H. Bornstein, eds. *Immigrant Families in Contemporary Society*. New York: Guilford Press, 2007.

Laslett, Barbara. "Personal Narratives as Sociology." *Contemporary Sociology* 28 (1999): 391–401.

Lawler, Veronica, ed. *I Was Dreaming to Come to America: Memories from the Ellis Island Oral History Project*. New York: Viking, 1995.

Lee, Erika. *At America's Gates: Chinese Immigration During the Exclusion Era, 1882–1943*. Chapel Hill: University of North Carolina Press, 2003.

Lee, Milly. *Landed*. New York: Farrar Straus Giroux, 2006.

Leighton, Maxine Rhea. *An Ellis Island Christmas*. New York: Viking, 1992.

Leverton, Bertha, and Shmuel Loewenson, eds. *I Came Alone: The Stories of the Kindertransports*. Sussex, UK: Book Guild, 1998.

Loughrey, Eithne. *Annie Moore: First in Line for America*. Dublin, Ireland: Mercier Press, 1999.

Maestro, Betsy. *Coming to America: The Story of Immigration*. New York: Scholastic, 1996.

Major, Aaron, and Ellen Alexander Conley. "Context and Immigrant Identity," in Ellen Alexander Conley, *The Chosen Shore: Stories of Immigrants*. Berkeley: University of California Press, 2004.

Martin, Philip, and Elizabeth Midgley. "Immigration: Shaping and Reshaping America." *Population Bulletin* 58, no. 2 (2003).

Miller, Donald E., and Lorna Touryan Miller. *Survivors: An Oral History of the Armenian Genocide*. Berkeley: University of California Press, 1993.

Mintz, Steven. *Huck's Raft: A History of American Childhood*. Cambridge, MA: Harvard University Press, 2004.

Moreno, Barry, *Children of Ellis Island*. Images of America. Charleston, SC: Arcadia Publishing, 2005.

———. *Ellis Island*. Images of America. Charleston, SC: Arcadia Publishing, 2003.

———. *Encyclopedia of Ellis Island*. Westport, CT: Greenwood Press, 2004.

Morrison, Joan, and Charlotte Fox Zabusky. *American Mosaic: The Immigrant Experience in the Words of Those Who Lived It*. New York: Dutton, 1980.

Portes, Alejandro, and Ruben G. Rumbaut. *Immigrant America: A Portrait*. Berkeley: University of California Press, 1996.

Ritchie, Donald A. *Doing Oral History: A Practical Guide*. New York: Oxford University Press, 2003.

Rumbaut, Ruben G., "Coming of Age in Immigrant America." *Research Perspectives on Migration* 6 (1998): 1–14.

———. "Ties That Bind." In Booth, Crouter, and Landale, *Immigration and the Family*, 29–42.

Sandler, Martin W. *Island of Hope: The Story of Ellis Island and the Journey to America*. New York: Scholastic, 2004.

Sheehy, Gail. *Spirit of Survival*. New York: William Morrow and Co., 1986.

Shields, Margie K., and R. Behrman. "Children of Immigrant Families: Analysis and Recommendations." *The Future of Children* 14 (Summer 2004): 4–14.

Short, Kathryn H., and Charlotte Johnston. "Stress, Maternal Distress, and Children's Adjustment Following Immigration: The Buffering Role of Social Support." *Journal of Consulting and Clinical Psychology* 65 (1997): 494–503.

Simon, Kate. *Bronx Primitive: Portraits of a Childhood.* New York: Harper & Row, 1982.

Suàrez-Orozco, Carola. "Immigrant Families and Their Children: Adaptation and Identity Formation." In *The Blackwell Companion to Sociology,* edited by Judith R. Blau, 128–39. Malden, MA: Blackwell, 2001.

Suàrez-Orozco, Carola, and Marcelo Suàrez-Orozco. *Children of Immigration.* Cambridge, MA: Harvard University Press, 2001.

Suàrez-Orozco, Carola, Marcelo Suàrez-Orozco, and Irina Todorova. *Learning in a New Land: Immigrant Students in America.* Cambridge, MA: Harvard University Press, 2008.

Werner, Emmy E. *Through the Eyes of Innocents: Children Witness World War II.* New York: Basic Books, 2000.

Werner, Emmy E., and Ruth S. Smith. *Journeys from Childhood to Midlife: Risk, Resilience, and Recovery.* Ithaca, NY: Cornell University Press, 2001.

Whitman, Sylvia. *Immigrant Children: Pictures of the American Past.* Minneapolis, MN: Carolrhoda Books, Inc., 2000.

Wyman, Mark. *DPs: Europe's Displaced Persons, 1945–1951.* Ithaca, NY: Cornell University Press, 1998.

Yans-McLaughlin, Virginia, and Marjorie Lightman. *Ellis Island and the Peopling of America: The Official Guide.* New York: New Press, 1997.

Zhou, Min. "Growing Up American: The Challenge Confronting Immigrant Children and Children of Immigrants." *Annual Review of Sociology* 23 (1997): 63–95.

About the Author

Emmy E. Werner is a developmental psychologist and research professor at the University of California at Davis. She has written extensively about contemporary children and children in history who have successfully overcome great adversities, such as political persecutions and the ravages of war. Werner is the author of *In Pursuit of Liberty: Coming of Age in the American Revolution, A Conspiracy of Decency: The Rescue of the Danish Jews During World War II, Through the Eyes of Innocents: Children Witness World War II, Reluctant Witnesses: Children's Voices from the Civil War,* and *Pioneer Children on the Journey West.* She lives in Berkeley, California.